KitchenAid

PASTRY
MADE EASY

1 MIXER, 80 RECIPES

KITCHENAID

MAKE MOMENTS UNFORGETTABLE

There's a reason why taco night stands out from all the nights spent rummaging through leftovers. There's a reason a good lunch can be enough to turn the whole day around. It's the same reason homemade appetizers earn more high fives than store-bought... it's because those meals and moments were made to stand out.

With KitchenAid, you make much more than food. You make weekend brunch look easy or make weeknight dinners next level. You can make to enjoy and make to impress. From shredding pork in the Stand Mixer to cranking out spaghetti with the Pasta Maker, trying out a recipe for soup in your Blender or serving up dips for a crowd with your Food Pro, and everything in between... when you've got KitchenAid on your countertop, you've got a secret weapon in making any meal memorable.

Turn on your KitchenAid appliance to discover a world of possibility.

FIND YOUR MIXER MATCH

1. SELECT A SIZE

3.3L
Master of dinner for two? Opt for the 'mini' version, which is also ideal for small kitchens.

4.8L
The iconic standard mixer, perfect for 4 to 6 people, whether friends or family.

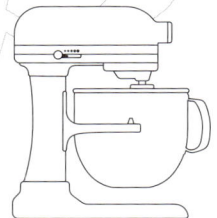

6.9L
Are you a master baker or someone with a big family to feed? Choose our Bowl-Lift model, inspired by professional design and applications.

2. PICK A COLOUR
Choose the colour that matches your personality.

3.3L	4.8L		6.9L
● Empire Red	● Candy Apple	● Fog Blue	● Candy Apple
● Matte Black	● Empire Red	● Blue Velvet	● Empire Red
● Almond Cream	● Onyx Black	● Ink Blue	● Onyx Black
● Matte Grey	● Cast Iron Black	○ Silk Pink	● Cast Iron Black
	● Almond Cream	● Dried Rose	○ White
	● Fresh Linen	● Feather Pink	● Dried Rose
	○ White	● Medallion Silver	● Medallion Silver
	● Pistachio	● Contour Silver	● Silver
	● Matcha	● Imperial Grey	
	● Pebbled Palm	● Chrome	
	● Kyoto Glow	● Brushed Nickel	
	● Majestic Yellow	● Copper	
	● Ice Blue	● Honey	

3. CHOOSE A BOWL

ACCESSORIES

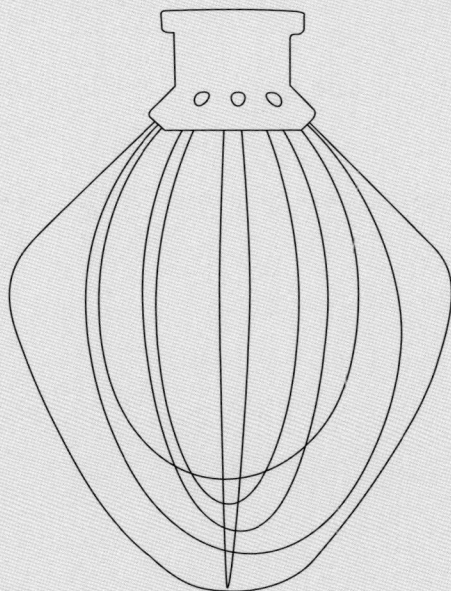

MIXER WHISK

USE

Begin by whisking on the lowest speed setting, then gradually increase the speed. If you whisk rapidly from the start, you risk incorporating less air into your mixes and the result will be heavier. You should also be careful to avoid using the whisk to work cold butter mixes as this may cause an unusable mass to collect in the middle of the whisk.

DISHES

The whisk allows you to beat air into mixtures to make:
- Beaten egg whites
- Meringues (see p. 18), etc.
- Savoury or sweet mousses: Floating islands (see p. 166), etc.
- Whipped cream (see p. 19)
- Sweet dishes: Raspberry macarons (see p. 128), Sundaes with dulce de leche (see p. 100), Vanilla and caramel millefeuille (see p. 194), etc.
- Savoury creations: Three-cheese soufflés (see p. 58), etc.

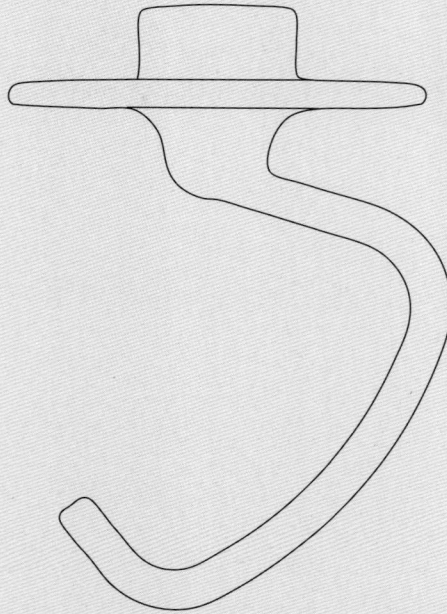

DOUGH HOOK

USE

Before attaching the dough hook to the mixer, mix all the dry ingredients in your recipe with the flat beater to evenly distribute them. Then use the dough hook as you gradually add the wet ingredients. Let the mixer run briefly to make a ball of dough. Continue kneading for a few minutes to make a smooth elastic dough, which you can then leave to rise in the bowl.

DISHES

The dough hook is your best friend for making superb dough and pastry-based creations including:
- Breads: Seeded multigrain bread (see p. 40), Cornbread (see p. 56), Brioche with pink pralines (see p. 30), Pains au lait (see p. 26), etc.
- Kneaded doughs: Puff pastry (see p. 17), Brioche dough (see p. 14), etc.
- Bread-based snacks: Salt bagels (see p. 70) or sweet bagels, Focaccia with olives (see p. 132), etc.

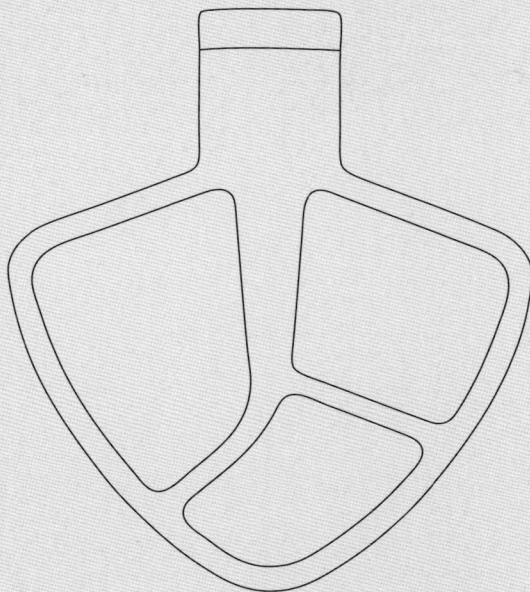

PADDLE ATTACHMENT

USE

As with the whisk, start running the paddle attachment on the lowest setting, then gradually increase the speed to the desired level. This will help to you avoid splatter and make uniform mixtures.

DISHES

The real go-to accessory for your Artisan mixer, you can use the paddle for any preparation that does not require using the whisk or dough hook.

It is ideal for making:
- Crumbles (see p. 104) and biscuits: Piped almond petits fours biscuits (see p. 120), Breton shortbread biscuits (see p. 122), etc.
- Cakes and breads: Pecan and salted butter caramel loaf cake (see p. 138), Pesto bread (see p. 72), Black Forest entremets (see p. 172), etc.
- Pastry for pies and tarts: Quiche Lorraine (see p. 86), Summer vegetable tart (see p. 82), etc.
- Choux pastry: Lemon and haddock gougères (see p. 84), etc.

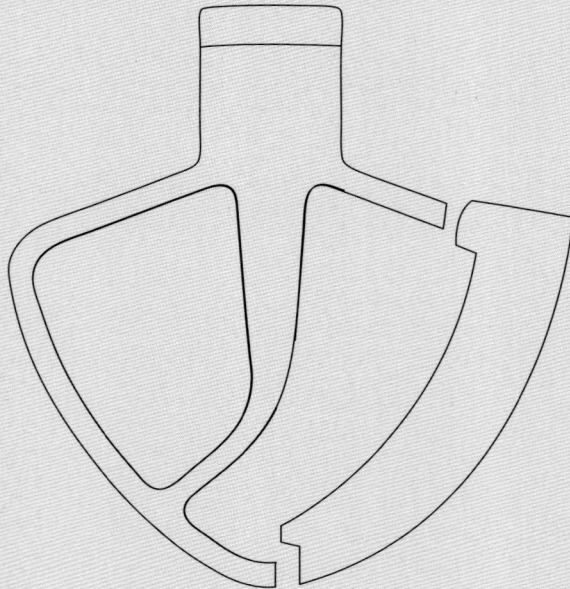

FLEX EDGE BEATER

USE

The flex edge beater allows you to thoroughly incorporate ingredients without having to stop the mixer or use a scraper. Its unique design smoothly scrapes down the sides of the bowl as it mixes, creating a perfect, quick and effortless result.

DISHES

It is useful for:
- All kinds of cakes and tarts: Chocolate tart (see p. 156), Banana bread (see p. 94), etc.
- Spreads (see p. 34).

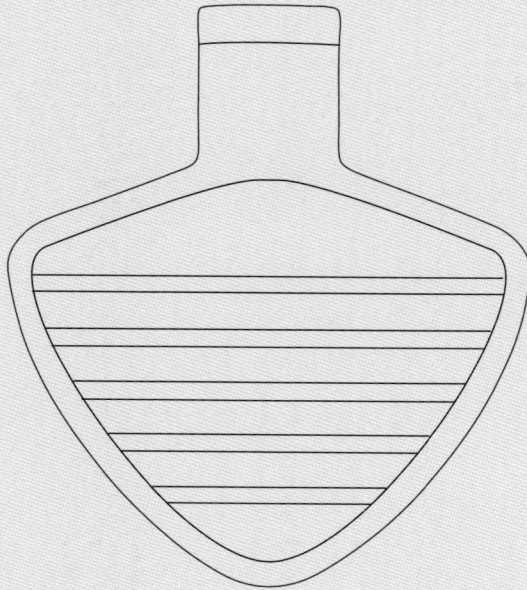

PASTRY BEATER

USE

The pastry beater allows you to easily incorporate cold butter into your preparations for creating artisan quality-dough. It is also ideal for puréeing cooked fruits or vegetables.

DISHES

It is very useful for:

- Making Shortbread pastry (see p. 15), Gourmet granola (see p. 42) and Cereal bars (see p. 134).
- Preparing savoury dishes: Pepper and feta loaf (p. 54), Savoury scones (see p. 62), etc.
- Puréeing cooked fruits and vegetables: Avocado toasts (see p. 78), Raspberry and white chocolate cupcakes (see p. 88), etc.
- Making cakes: Carrot cupcakes (see p. 96), Pecan brownies (see p. 140), Baked lemon cheesecake (see p. 142), etc.

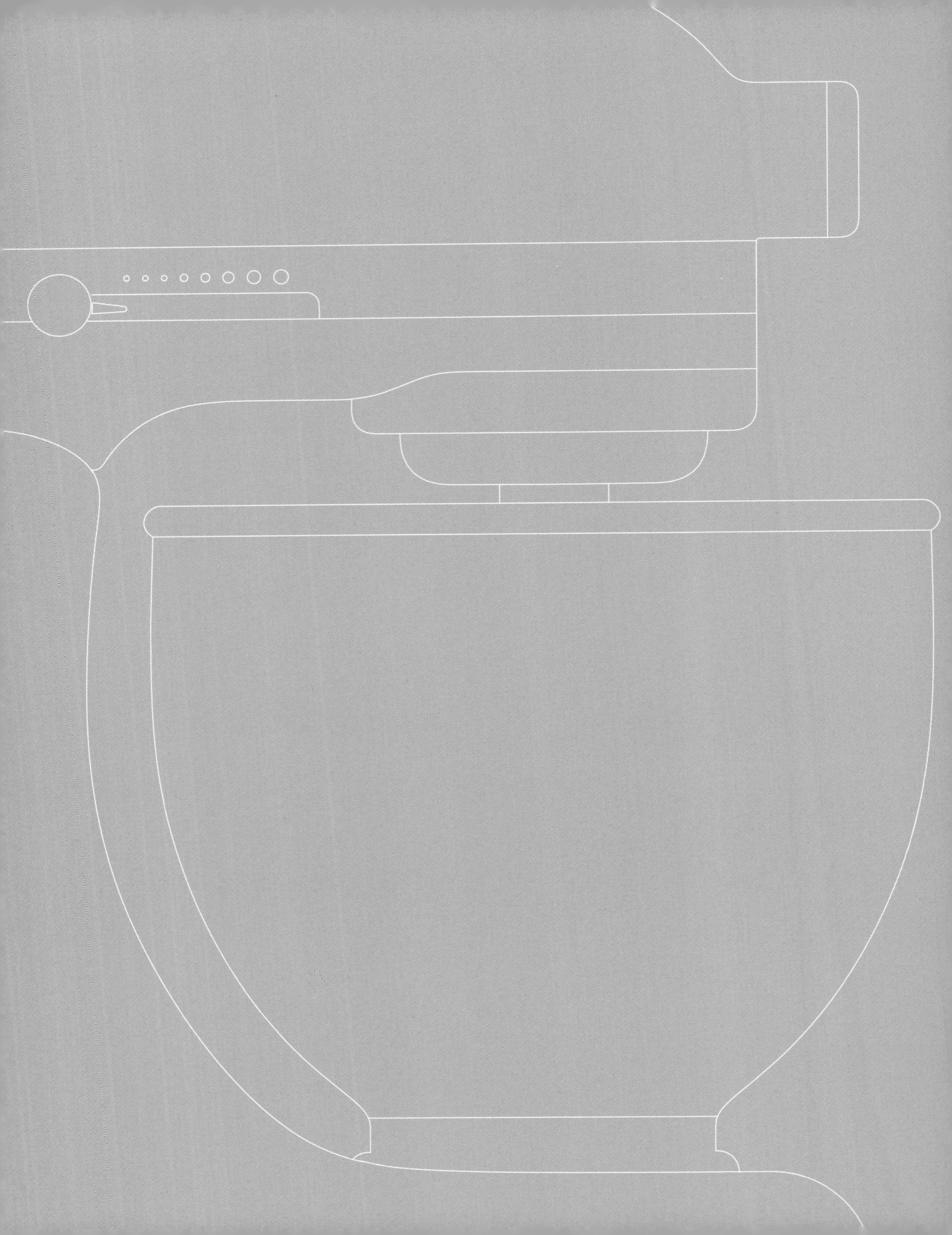

BASIC RECIPES

BRIOCHE DOUGH

02

FOR THE DOUGH

01. Put the beaten eggs into the mixer fitted with the dough hook. Crumble the yeast into the eggs for better distribution. Add the flour, sugar and salt. Knead the dough on speed 1 for 2 minutes.

02. Dust the bowl and dough hook with flour and scrape. Knead the dough on speed 2 for 3 minutes, then on speed 4 for 3 minutes. When the dough pulls away from sides of the bowl and forms a ball, reduce the speed to 1 and add the softened butter, cut into small cubes.

03. Knead the dough on speed 1 for 2 minutes, then on speed 3 for 3 minutes, until it pulls away from the sides of the bowl.

● INFO

Scrape means to use a bowl scraper to remove any dough or mixture from any utensil or the sides of a container.

Makes 6 brioches (25 x 10 cm)

Preparation time: 25 minutes

Resting time: 1 hour 45 minutes

200 g (4) eggs
15 g fresh yeast
330 g strong white flour
60 g caster sugar
7 g fine salt
170 g unsalted butter

CHOUX PASTRY

02

01. In a saucepan, heat 150 g of water with the milk, salt and butter, cut into small pieces. When the mixture comes to the boil, remove from the heat and add the sifted flour all at once.

02. Mix briskly until the resulting paste forms a smooth, lump-free ball. The paste should be a little dry, so don't hesitate to return the saucepan to the heat while you mix.

03. Transfer the paste to the mixer fitted with the paddle attachment. Start the mixer on speed 1, then add the beaten eggs in four or five batches. Increase to speed 2 and mix until smooth. Take care towards the end: the choux paste should be soft but able to hold its shape, neither too dry nor too runny. It should form a peak at the end of the paddle.

Makes about 60 small choux buns

Preparation time: 10 minutes

100 g semi-skimmed milk
5 g salt
100 g unsalted butter
150 g plain flour
240 g (4 large or 5 small) eggs

SWEET SHORTCRUST PASTRY

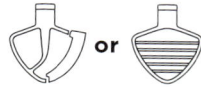

Makes 1 tart

Preparation time: 10 minutes

Resting time: 1 hour

100 g unsalted butter, softened
70 g icing sugar
1 pinch salt
35 g egg
175 g plain flour
30 g ground almonds

01. Put the softened butter into the mixer fitted with the flex edge beater or pastry beater and mix on speed 4 for 3 minutes.

02. Add the sugar and salt and mix on speed 4 for 2 minutes, then add the egg while continuing to mix. Finally, reduce to speed 2 and incorporate the flour and ground almonds.

03. Form the dough into a ball, wrap in cling film and refrigerate for 1 hour.

04. Roll out the dough on a floured work surface and line a tart tin greased with butter and flour.

03

SHORTBREAD PASTRY

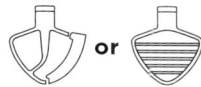

Serves 8

Preparation time: 5 minutes

Resting time: 30 minutes

250 g plain flour
40 g caster sugar
3 pinches salt
125 g unsalted butter
1 egg

01. In the mixer fitted with the pastry or paddle beater attachment, combine the flour, sugar and salt on speed 1 for 30 seconds.

02. Add the butter, cut into cubes, and increase to speed 2 for 2 minutes. Finally, add the egg and mix until the dough just forms a ball.

03. Wrap the dough in cling film and refrigerate for 30 minutes.

03

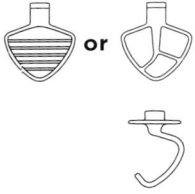

SHORTCRUST PASTRY

01. In the mixer fitted with the pastry beater attachment or the paddle, combine the flour, salt and butter, cut into cubes, on speed 2 for about 2 minutes.

02. Once the mixture has a sandy texture, replace the paddle with the dough hook. Add the water, a little at a time, while kneading on speed 2.

03. Once the dough is smooth, use your hands to shape it into a ball. Wrap the dough in cling film and refrigerate for at least 30 minutes.

Serves 6–8 (makes 1 tart/ 20 cm in diameter)

Preparation time: 10 minutes

Resting time: 30 minutes

200 g plain flour
2 g salt
100 g unsalted butter
35 g lukewarm water

PUFF PASTRY

Makes 1 tart (275 g pastry)

Preparation time: 45 minutes

Resting time: 2 hours

250 g plain flour
¼ tsp salt
90 g dry butter

01. In the mixer fitted with the dough hook, add the flour, salt and 60 g of water. Mix on speed 2 and knead for 5 minutes until a smooth dough forms.

02. Remove the dough from the mixer, wrap in cling film and refrigerate for at least 30 minutes.

03. In the meantime, soften the butter by pounding it with a rolling pin. Shape it into a square. Roll out the dough into a long rectangle, place the butter in the middle and fold the edges over.

04. Give the dough a quarter turn to the right, roll out into a long rectangle and fold into thirds, letter style. Give it another quarter turn, again to the right. Roll out again into a long rectangle, then fold again into thirds, letter style.

05. Refrigerate the dough for 30 minutes. Repeat this process two more times.

⬤ **TIPS**

Once the puff pastry is ready, you can use it to make tart cases, millefeuilles, turnovers, etc. It can also be frozen.

CUSTARD (CRÈME ANGLAISE)

01. In the mixer fitted with the whisk, mix the egg yolks with the sugar on speed 4 for 3 minutes.

02. In the meantime, heat the milk. Mix well. While continuing to mix, pour the boiling milk, a little at a time, into the mixer bowl.

03. Return the mixture to the saucepan and cook over a low heat, stirring constantly with a wooden spoon, until it begins to thicken. Once the custard coats the back of the spoon, remove from the heat. Leave to cool and then refrigerate.

⬤ **TIP**

Flavour the custard however you like: with pistachio paste, orange flower water, vanilla, cinnamon, praline, chocolate, home-made spread, etc.

SERVES 4–6
Preparation time: 5 minutes
Cooking time: 5 minutes

6 egg yolks
100 g caster sugar
500 ml semi-skimmed milk

ITALIAN MERINGUE

01. Mix 60 g of water with the sugar in a saucepan. Put the egg whites into the mixer fitted with the whisk.

02. Place the saucepan over the heat to make a syrup. When the temperature of the syrup reaches 110°C, start beating the egg whites on speed 8. Heat the syrup to 121°C.

03. Reduce the mixer speed to 4, then pour the syrup, a little at a time, over the partially beaten egg whites. Turn the speed back up to 8 and whisk until the meringue cools completely.

Makes 450 g meringue
Preparation time: 20 minutes

300 g caster sugar
180 g (6) egg whites

WHIPPED CREAM

Preparation time: 2 minutes

1 litre whipping cream

01. In the mixer fitted with the whisk, whip the very cold cream on speed 8 for 1 minute 30 seconds–2 minutes.

PASTRY CREAM

Makes 650 g pastry cream
Preparation time: 10 minutes
Cooking time: 5 minutes
Resting time: 1 hour

55 g caster sugar
50 g cornflour
100 g (2 small) eggs
500 g semi-skimmed milk
1 vanilla pod or 1 tsp vanilla powder
1 pinch salt
1 knob unsalted butter

01. In the mixer fitted with the whisk, combine 35 g of the sugar with the cornflour and eggs. Start the mixer on speed 2, then gradually increase to speed 6.

02. In a saucepan, heat the milk with the remaining 20 g of sugar and the seeds from the vanilla pod until it just comes to the boil. Reduce the mixer speed to 1 and gradually pour the boiling milk into the bowl. Whisk for about 1 minute.

03. Return the mixture to the saucepan and bring to the boil, whisking constantly. Leave to cook for another minute, stirring constantly. Remove from the heat and add the salt and butter. Mix, then transfer to a dish and cover with cling film in direct contact with the cream. Refrigerate for at least 1 hour.

BREAKFAST

LIÈGE WAFFLES

Warm the milk and dissolve the yeast. Set aside.

In the mixer fitted with the dough hook, add the flour, salt and raw sugar, then mix on speed 1 for 1 minute. Add the egg, followed by the milk and yeast mixture and the butter. Mix on speed 1 for 2 minutes, then increase to speed 2 for 8 minutes. Cover the bowl with a clean cloth and rest for 1 hour at room temperature.

Add the pearl sugar and mix again to incorporate into the dough. Shape the dough into small balls, place on a rack and rest for a further 30 minutes.

Heat the waffle maker. Cook the dough balls in the waffle maker for about 2 minutes. Serve them Brussels style with brown sugar.

125 g semi-skimmed milk
24 g fresh yeast
300 g plain flour
1 pinch fine salt
30 g raw sugar
1 small egg
200 g unsalted butter, at room temperature
200 g pearl (nib) sugar

SERVES 4-6

Preparation
time:
30 minutes

Cooking time:
2 minutes

Resting time:
1 hour
30 minutes

PARISIAN BRIOCHE

FOR THE DOUGH
Make the brioche dough as described on p. 14.

RISING
Take the dough out of the mixer and shape it into a ball. Place it in a bowl and cover with cling film in direct contact. Leave to rise at room temperature for 1 hour. Knead the dough to deflate it, then roll into a ball. Wrap the dough with cling film. Refrigerate for 2 hours.

SHAPING
On a work surface, deflate and then shape the dough into a ball. Rest at room temperature for 5 minutes. Reshape into a ball and refrigerate for 10 minutes.
Using the edge of your hand, press into the dough with a sawing motion to shape the dough ball into two parts: a smaller 'head' and a larger 'body'.
Grease a brioche mould by brushing it with butter, and centre the brioche in the mould. Dust your forefinger with flour and push it down to the base of the mould around the body of the brioche to position it well. Brush the top of the brioche with the beaten egg, taking care not to let any drip down the sides.

PROVING
Place the mould on the oven baking tray and prove the brioche in an improvised proving oven at 24°C for 2 hours (see opposite).

BAKING
Take the brioche out of the oven and rest at room temperature for 10 minutes. Preheat the oven to 200°C (Gas Mark 6) with the baking tray inside. Glaze the brioche again.
Place the brioche mould on the hot baking tray and bake at 180°C (Gas Mark 4) for 15–18 minutes. After taking the brioche out of the oven, turn it out of the mould, then put it back inside the still-hot mould for 2 minutes to lightly dry out the bottom. Then leave to cool on a rack.

200 g (4) eggs
15 g fresh yeast
330 g Italian '00' flour or plain flour
60 g caster sugar
7 g fine salt
170 g unsalted butter
1 beaten egg, for glazing

TIP

Brioche dough is normally proved in a proving oven. It is very easy to improvise and turn your oven into one without having to switch it on. Boil 1 litre of water, pour it into a baking dish and place it at the bottom of the oven. Position the oven rack in the middle position, place the brioche on it and close the oven door. Prove the brioche for 1–2 hours, depending on the recipe. Then take the brioche out of the oven. Don't forget to take out the dish of water. You can now use the oven to bake the brioche.

For 1 large
brioche

Preparation
time:
45 minutes

Cooking time:
20 minutes

Resting time:
5 hours
25 minutes

PAINS AU LAIT

FOR THE PAIN AU LAIT DOUGH

In the mixer fitted with the dough hook, add the flour, salt, sugar, milk powder, eggs, honey, 170 g of water and the yeast. Run the mixer on speed 2 for 5 minutes, to mix the dough until smooth and free of lumps.

Increase to speed 4 and knead for about 5 minutes to add elasticity to the dough.

Reduce the speed to 2 and add the butter, cut into small pieces. When incorporated, increase the speed to 4 for 3 minutes. The dough should pull away from the sides of the bowl and form a ball around the dough hook.

Transfer the dough to a bowl and cover with cling film. Leave to rise for 1 hour at room temperature. This step is known as rising.

Flatten the dough to deflate it, then refrigerate it for 30 minutes.

FINISHING

Divide and weigh out the dough into 60-g pieces. Lightly flour the work surface. Flatten the dough portions by folding and pressing with the palm of your hand. Repeat the action two or three times. Gradually stretch out the dough by pushing it outwards with the heel of your hand to form sausage-shaped buns 15 cm long.

Arrange the buns on a baking tray lined with baking parchment. Glaze by brushing with the beaten egg. Prove in the oven at 30°C for 1 hour 45 minutes (see p. 24).

Take out the proved dough and rest for 10 minutes at room temperature. Preheat the oven to 180°C (Gas Mark 4). Glaze the buns again. Dip the tip of a pair of scissors in cold water to ensure a clean cut, then make snips over the top of the buns. Sprinkle with pearl sugar. Put the buns into the oven, lower the temperature to 170°C (Gas Mark 3½) and bake for 12 minutes. Transfer to a rack to cool.

FOR THE PAIN AU LAIT DOUGH

500 g Italian '00' flour or plain flour

10 g salt

50 g caster sugar

25 g full-fat milk powder

100 g (2) eggs

10 g honey

15 g fresh yeast

100 g unsalted butter

FINISHING

1 beaten egg, for glazing

150 g pearl (nib) sugar

DID YOU KNOW?

Strong white flour is used for leavened doughs because it is higher in gluten, which is what gives the dough its elasticity.

Makes 850 g dough

Preparation time: 45 minutes

Cooking time: 12 minutes

Resting time: 3 hours 25 minutes

PAINS AUX RAISINS

5

FOR THE PASTRY CREAM

Combine the milk, scraped vanilla seeds and half the sugar in a saucepan over the heat. In a bowl, blanch the egg yolks by whisking them with the remaining sugar until thick and pale. Mix in the custard powder. When the milk comes to the boil, mix a small amount into the blanched egg yolks. Then return the mixture to the pan. Cook for 4 minutes over a low heat, stirring constantly, until the cream thickens. Transfer to a large dish and cover with cling film in direct contact. Set aside for about 1 hour in the refrigerator or 20 minutes in the freezer.

FOR THE PAIN AU LAIT DOUGH

Make the pain au lait dough as described on p. 26 using the quantities given here.

FINISHING

Soak the raisins in a container of boiling water for 30 minutes.

On baking parchment, gently roll out the dough into a 40 x 30-cm rectangle. Brush a strip of beaten egg along one of the shorter edges of the rectangle.
Mix the pastry cream until very smooth. Use an angled palette knife to spread the pastry cream over the dough, leaving the strip of beaten egg uncovered. Drain the raisins and scatter them over the cream. Roll up the dough along its long edge into a uniform cylinder. Freeze for 20 minutes.

Cut the roll into 3-cm-thick discs. Glaze the discs by brushing them with the beaten egg. Prove in the oven at 30°C (see p. 24).

Take out the pains aux raisins and rest for 10 minutes at room temperature. Preheat the oven to 180°C (Gas Mark 4). Glaze the pains aux raisins again. Put them into the oven, lower the temperature to 170°C (Gas Mark 3½) and bake for 12 minutes. Transfer to a rack to cool.

FOR THE PASTRY CREAM

200 g milk

1 vanilla pod

15 g caster sugar

30 g (2 small) egg yolks

15 g custard powder

FOR THE PAIN AU LAIT DOUGH

250 g Italian '00' flour or plain flour

5 g salt

25 g caster sugar

12 g full-fat milk powder

50 g (1) egg

5 g honey

85 g water

7 g fresh yeast

50 g unsalted butter

FINISHING

100 g raisins

1 beaten egg, for glazing

TIPS

You can use chocolate chips instead of raisins, and you can flavour the custard with pistachio paste. If you like, you can also brush the freshly baked pains aux raisins with syrup to make them glossy.

Makes
10 pains
aux raisins

Preparation
time:
1 hour

Cooking time:
12 minutes

Resting time:
3 hours
35 minutes

BRIOCHE WITH PINK PRALINES

FOR THE DOUGH

The previous day, put the eggs and milk into the mixer fitted with the dough hook. Crumble the yeast over this mixture for better diffusion. Add the lemon zest, followed by the flour, sugar and salt. Knead on speed 1 for 3 minutes, then increase to speed 2 and knead for a further 3 minutes.

When the dough pulls away from sides of the bowl and forms a ball, add the softened butter, cut into small cubes. Knead the dough on speed 1 for 6 minutes, then increase to speed 4 for 2 minutes, until the butter is incorporated and the dough pulls away from the sides of the bowl in a smooth ball.

Add the chopped pralines and mix on speed 1 until well incorporated.

RISING

Take the dough out of the mixer and shape it into a ball. Place it in a bowl and cover with cling film in direct contact. Leave to rise at room temperature for 2 hours. Deflate and then shape the dough into a ball. Wrap it in cling film. Refrigerate for 12 hours.

SHAPING THE BRIOCHE

The next day, deflate and then shape it the dough into a ball. Rest at room temperature for 5 minutes.

Grease a cake ring with butter and line it with a strip of baking parchment. Place the cake ring on baking parchment. Put the dough into the centre of the cake ring and flatten with the back of your hand. Brush the top of the brioche with the beaten egg, taking care not to let any drip down the sides.

PROVING

Prove the brioche in an improvised proving oven at 24°C for 2 hours (see p. 24).

BAKING AND FINISHING

Take the brioche out of the oven and rest at room temperature for 10 minutes. Preheat the oven to 180°C (Gas Mark 4) with the oven baking tray inside. Glaze the brioche again and sprinkle with pearl sugar.

Place the brioche on the hot baking tray and bake at 170°C (Gas Mark 3½) for 30–35 minutes.

Carefully transfer the brioche with the brioche ring to a rack. Once it has cooled down, lift off the cake ring.

FOR THE BRIOCHE DOUGH

75 g (2 small) eggs

62 g milk

11 g fresh yeast

Zest of 1 lemon

250 g Italian '00' flour or plain flour

15 g caster sugar

6 g fine salt

100 g unsalted butter, softened

100 g pink pralines, chopped

1 beaten egg, for glazing

FINISHING

Pearl (nib) sugar

TIP

You can brush the top of the freshly baked brioche with a neutral syrup to make it glossy.

Makes 1 large
brioche

Preparation
time:
45 minutes

Cooking time:
35 minutes

Resting time:
16 hours
10 minutes

BRIOCHE TWIST WITH SPREAD FILLING

FOR THE DOUGH
Make the brioche dough as described on p. 14.

RISING
Take the dough out of the mixer and shape it into a ball. Place it in a bowl and cover with cling film in direct contact. Leave to rise at room temperature for 1 hour. Deflate and then shape the dough into a ball and wrap it in cling film. Refrigerate for 2 hours.

SHAPING
Deflate the dough with the palm of your hand. With a rolling pin, roll out the dough into a 40 × 60-cm rectangle. Cover the entire surface of the dough with the spread. Roll up the dough along its short edge. Wrap in cling film and refrigerate for 30 minutes.
Use a large knife to cut the roll in half lengthways. Twist the two half rolls together, making sure to leave the spread filling visible. Cut the twist in half across its middle and then place the brioches into two loaf tins greased with butter.

PROVING
Place the brioches in their tins on the oven baking tray and prove in an improvised proving oven at 24°C for 2 hours (see p. 24).

FOR THE ICING
Split the vanilla pod in half and scrape out the seeds with the tip of a small knife. Combine the seeds with the milk in a bowl. Sift the icing sugar. Gradually whisk the vanilla-infused milk into the icing sugar. Add more milk or icing sugar if needed to achieve the desired consistency. Cover with cling film and refrigerate.

BAKING AND FINISHING
Take the brioches out of the oven and rest at room temperature for 10 minutes. Preheat the oven to 180°C (Gas Mark 4) with the baking tray inside. Place the brioches on the hot baking tray and bake at 170°C (Gas Mark 3½) for 15–18 minutes.
Brush the brioches with the sugar icing while they are still hot. Leave to cool a little before turning them out and then transfer to a rack.

FOR THE BRIOCHE DOUGH
200 g (4) eggs
15 g fresh yeast
330 g Italian '00' flour or plain flour
60 g caster sugar
7 g fine salt
170 g unsalted butter

FOR THE FILLING
1 x 250-g jar spread of your choice

FOR THE SUGAR ICING
½ vanilla pod
45 g milk
150 g icing sugar

TIP Use the spread suggested on p. 34.

Makes
2 medium
brioche
twists

Preparation
time:
50 minutes

Cooking time:
18 minutes

Resting time:
5 hours
40 minutes

HAZELNUT SPREAD

Preheat the oven to 180°C (Gas Mark 4). Put the hazelnuts onto a baking sheet lined with baking parchment. Roast for 15 minutes in the oven, stirring halfway through. The hazelnuts should turn a deep golden brown. Blend to a smooth paste.

Heat the cream in a saucepan. Add the dark chocolate and milk chocolate, broken into pieces, leave to stand for 3 minutes and then mix until smooth.

Put the hazelnut butter into the mixer fitted with the flex edge beater. Add the chocolate cream, icing sugar, oil and vanilla extract. Mix on speed 4 for 2 minutes. Transfer the mixture to two jars and seal securely. Keep in the refrigerator and use within 15 days.

200 g hazelnuts
150 ml whipping cream
100 g dark chocolate
100 g milk chocolate
40 g icing sugar
2 tbsp neutral oil (groundnut or grapeseed)
1 tsp vanilla extract

TIPS

You can add a pinch of fleur
de sel. Use any nuts you like: almonds, cashews, macadamia nuts, etc. You can also replace the neutral oil with coconut oil.

Makes 2 jars

Preparation
time:
10 minutes

Cooking time:
15 minutes

CHOCOLATE SWIRL BRIOCHE

FOR THE PLAIN BRIOCHE DOUGH

The previous day, put the egg with 210 g of water into the mixer fitted with the dough hook. Crumble the yeast into the water and egg for better distribution. Add the flour, milk powder, sugar and salt. Knead on speed 1 for 5 minutes, then increase to speed 2 and knead for 5 minutes.

When the dough pulls away from sides of the bowl and forms a ball, add the softened butter, cut into small cubes. Knead the dough on speed 2 for 5 minutes, until the butter is incorporated and the dough pulls away from the sides of the bowl in a smooth ball.

RISING

Weigh out and set aside 250 g of the plain brioche dough. Shape the rest of the dough into a ball. Place in a bowl and cover with cling film in direct contact. Leave to rise in the refrigerator for 12 hours.

FOR THE CHOCOLATE BRIOCHE DOUGH

In the mixer fitted with the dough hook, add the dough with the cocoa powder, 20 g of water and the butter. Knead on speed 1 for 5 minutes. Stop when the dough pulls away from the sides of the bowl and forms a smooth ball.

RISING

Take the dough out of the mixer and shape into a ball. Place in a bowl and cover with cling film in direct contact. Leave to rise in the refrigerator for 12 hours.

On the actual day, deflate the plain brioche dough. With a rolling pin, roll out the dough into a 40 × 20-cm rectangle.
Deflate the chocolate brioche dough. Roll out the dough into a 40 × 20 cm rectangle. Brush the chocolate dough with the beaten egg.
Lay the plain dough on top of the chocolate dough. Roll up the two doughs along their short edge with the chocolate dough always on the outside. Brush the roll with beaten egg and score with a lame (baker's blade or grignette). Cut the roll in half across the middle.
Place the rolls in two loaf tins greased with butter.

PROVING

Prove the brioches in an improvised proving oven at 24°C for 2 hours (see p. 24).

FOR THE PLAIN BRIOCHE DOUGH

40 g (1 small) egg

20 g fresh yeast

375 g Italian '00' flour or plain flour

8 g milk powder

60 g caster sugar

8 g fine salt

75 g unsalted butter, softened

FOR THE CHOCOLATE BRIOCHE DOUGH

250 g plain brioche dough

25 g cocoa powder

10 g unsalted butter

1 beaten egg, for glazing

FOR THE SYRUP

135 g caster sugar

Makes
2 medium
brioches

Preparation
time:
50 minutes

Cooking time:
25 minutes

Resting time:
12 hours +
12 hours +
2 hours

FOR THE SYRUP

Put 100 g of water into a saucepan. Mix in the sugar. Bring to the boil to fully dissolve the sugar.

BAKING AND FINISHING

Take the brioches out of the oven and rest at room temperature for 10 minutes.

Preheat the oven to 180°C (Gas Mark 4) with the oven baking tray inside. Place the brioches on the hot baking tray and bake at 170°C (Gas Mark 3½) for 10 minutes, then at 150°C (Gas Mark 2) for 15 minutes.

Glaze the freshly baked brioches with the syrup. When they have cooled a little, turn them out and transfer to a rack.

BUCHTY
BRIOCHE
WITH MASCARPONE

FOR THE DOUGH
Make the brioche dough as described on p. 14.

RISING
Take the dough out of the mixer and shape it into a
ball. Place it in a bowl and cover with cling film in direct
contact. Leave to rise at room temperature for 2 hours.
Knead the dough to deflate it, then shape it into a ball
and wrap in cling film. Refrigerate for 2 hours.

SHAPING THE BRIOCHE
Deflate and then divide and weigh out the dough into
sixteen 40-g pieces. Shape the individual pieces into
balls by rolling them with the palm of your hand on the
work surface. Grease a square baking frame with butter
and place on baking parchment. Arrange the dough
balls inside the frame in four rows of four.
Brush the top of the brioche with the beaten egg, taking care not to let any drip down the sides.

PROVING
Prove the brioche in an improvised proving oven at
24°C for 2 hours (see p. 24).

BAKING AND FINISHING
Take the brioche out of the oven and rest at room
temperature for 10 minutes. Preheat the oven to 180°C
(Gas Mark 4) with the oven baking tray inside. Place
the brioches on the hot baking tray and bake at 165°C
(Gas Mark 3) for 15–18 minutes.
Carefully transfer the brioche with the baking frame
to a rack. Once it has cooled down somewhat, lift off
the baking frame.

70 g (2 small) eggs
15 g fresh yeast
2 vanilla pods
70 g semi-skimmed milk
170 g mascarpone cheese
**335 g Italian '00' flour
or plain flour**
40 g caster sugar
7 g fine salt
1 beaten egg, for glazing

For 1 medium
brioche

Preparation
time:
45 minutes

Cooking time:
18 minutes

Resting time:
6 hours
10 minutes

SEEDED MULTIGRAIN BREAD

FOR THE DOUGH

In the mixer fitted with the dough hook, add the luke-warm water and the yeast. Knead on speed 1 for 30 seconds to dissolve the yeast. Add the different flours, 75 g of the seed mix and the salt. Increase to speed 2 and knead for 10 minutes. Shape the dough into a ball, cover with a cloth and leave to rise in the mixer bowl in a warm place for 40 minutes.

When the dough has risen, use a palette knife to transfer it to the work surface and knead by hand for 5 minutes. Shape the dough into a ball again and place on a baking tray lined with baking parchment. Sprinkle with the remaining seed mix. Prove for 1 hour 30 minutes in a warm place.

BAKING

Preheat the oven to 200°C (Gas Mark 6). Place a bowl of water on the lower oven shelf to help a crust develop during baking. Bake for 25 minutes, then reduce the oven temperature to 180°C (Gas Mark 4) and bake for a further 15–20 minutes. Leave the loaf to cool before slicing.

450 ml lukewarm water

10 g active dried yeast

450 g strong bread flour

150 g rye flour

75 g semi-wholemeal (French type-80) flour

150 g seed mix (pumpkin, sunflower, poppy, etc.)

7.5 g salt

VARIATIONS

You can also use prepared multigrain flour mixes. You can replace the dried yeast with 20 g of fresh yeast.

Serves 6

Preparation
time:
15 minutes

Cooking time:
45 minutes

Resting time:
2 hours
10 minutes

GOURMET GRANOLA

Preheat the oven to 150°C (Gas Mark 2). Chop the hazelnuts and almonds with a knife. In the mixer fitted with the pastry beater, add the oats, chopped nuts, sunflower seeds and salt.

In a small saucepan, melt the coconut oil with the honey. Run the mixer on speed 2 and add the oil mixture. Mix for 2 minutes, then spread over a baking tray lined with baking parchment. Bake for 15–20 minutes, stirring halfway through. Keep a close eye on the granola as it bakes because it browns quickly. Leave the granola to cool and harden. Finally, stir in the chocolate chips. Store in an airtight jar. Serve with almond milk.

50 g hazelnuts
50 g almonds
250 g porridge oats
2 tbsp sunflower seeds
1 pinch salt
2 tbsp coconut oil
4 tbsp honey
100 g chocolate chips

VARIATIONS

You can use a mixture of grain flakes (rice, quinoa, chestnut, buckwheat, etc.) Vary the nuts and grains according to your preference (macadamia nuts, pine nuts, pistachios, linseed, sesame seeds, etc.) You can also flavour the granola with vanilla or cinnamon. If you don't like the taste of coconut oil, replace it with walnut, hazelnut or grapeseed oil. You can also replace the honey with agave syrup or maple syrup. Ready-to-use almond milk can be bought in most supermarkets.

DRY TOASTS

FOR THE DOUGH
Dissolve the yeast and sugar in the lukewarm water. Leave to foam for about 10 minutes.

Combine the milk and butter in a saucepan and lightly warm.

In the mixer fitted with the paddle attachment, combine the flour, guar gum and salt. Add the egg, butter-milk mixture, olive oil and yeast-sugar mixture. Mix on speed 1 for 2 minutes, until a smooth dough forms. Put the dough into a loaf tin lined with baking parchment. Cover with a damp cloth and rest in a warm place for 1 hour.

BAKING
Preheat the oven to 180°C (Gas Mark 4). Bake for 40 minutes, then turn out and leave to cool.

Cut the loaf into slices about 1 cm thick and place them directly on the oven rack. Bake at 100°C (Gas Mark ¼) for 40 minutes–1 hour, depending on the desired level of crispness.

5 g active dried yeast
1 tsp cane sugar
50 ml lukewarm water
100 ml milk
10 g unsalted butter
180 g gluten-free bread flour
1 tsp guar gum
1 pinch salt
1 egg
1 tbsp olive oil

TIPS

You can use a plant-based milk (almond, hazelnut, rice, soya, etc.) instead of cow's milk. For more flavourful toast, replace 30 g of the bread flour with chestnut or buckwheat flour.

Makes about
20 slices of
dry toast

Preparation
time:
20 minutes

Cooking time:
1 hour
25 minutes–
1 hour
45 minutes

Resting time:
1 hour

GLUTEN-FREE BRIOCHE

FOR THE DOUGH

Lightly heat the milk, pour it into a bowl and add the 1 teaspoon of sugar and the yeast. Leave to foam for about 10 minutes. In the meantime, melt the butter. Beat the eggs with a fork.

In the mixer fitted with the pastry beater, add the flour, ground almonds, the remaining sugar, the guar gum and salt. Mix on speed 1 for 1 minute. Add the melted butter, milk with the yeast, beaten eggs and orange flower water. Mix on speed 1 for 1 minute, then increase to speed 2 for 3 minutes.

SHAPING

Divide the dough into quarters. Flour your hands well and shape the dough into 4 balls of equal size. Arrange the balls close together in a loaf tin lined with baking parchment. Cover with a damp cloth and leave to rise for 1 hour in a warm place.

BAKING

Preheat the oven to 180°C (Gas Mark 4).
Brush the brioche with milk. Bake for 30 minutes and leave to cool before slicing.

200 ml milk

1 tsp + 40 g cane sugar

5 g active dried yeast

50 g unsalted butter

2 eggs

200 g gluten-free bread flour

50 g ground almonds

1 tsp guar gum

1 tsp salt

1 tbsp orange flower water

VARIATIONS

You can also use almond milk for this recipe. For a more indulgent version, add 100 g of chocolate chips to the dough.

**Makes
1 brioche**

**Preparation
time:
20 minutes**

**Cooking time:
30 minutes**

**Resting time:
1 hour**

FRENCH GINGERBREAD

Preheat the oven to 180°C (Gas Mark 4).

Heat the milk in a saucepan, then add the butter and honey. As soon as the mixture starts to boil, remove from the heat.

In the mixer fitted with the pastry beater, combine the flour and ground almonds. Add the baking powder, bicarbonate of soda, salt, brown sugar and spices. Mix on speed 1 for 1 minute. Then pour in the milk-honey mixture and mix on speed 1 for 1 minute before increasing to speed 2 for 1 minute. Add the egg and marmalade and mix on speed 2 for 2 minutes.

Grease a loaf tin with butter and dust it with flour. Pour the batter into the tin and put it into the oven. Bake for 40 minutes. Turn out the gingerbread and leave to cool before slicing.

100 ml milk
60 g unsalted butter
200 g honey
250 g plain flour
60 g ground almonds
11 g baking powder
1 pinch bicarbonate of soda
1 pinch salt
50 g brown sugar
1 tsp quatre-épices spice blend
1 tsp ground ginger
1 tsp cinnamon
1 egg
40 g orange marmalade

PAINS AU CHOCOLAT

FOR THE DOUGH
In the mixer fitted with the dough hook, add the flour, sugar, salt, softened butter and yeast. Knead on speed 1 for 5 minutes, adding the milk a little at a time. Increase to speed 2 and knead for 3 minutes, until the dough forms a ball. Wrap in cling film and refrigerate for 1 hour.

TURNING (FOLDING)
Roll out the dough into a 60 x 30-cm rectangle. Roll out the chilled butter between two sheets of baking parchment into a 25-cm square. Lay the butter on half of the dough and fold over the other half to cover. Seal the edges of the resulting square. Rotate the dough by a quarter turn (90 degrees), then roll it out into a 6-mm-thick rectangle. Fold the two shorter ends into the centre of the rectangle and then fold it in half: the result will be four layers. Wrap the dough in cling film and refrigerate for 1 hour.

Roll out the dough, with the folds to the right, to make a 6-mm-thick rectangle. Then fold it in three. Wrap it in cling film and refrigerate for 1 hour. Repeat the process, wrap in cling film and refrigerate for 1 hour.

Roll out the dough into a large 4-mm-thick square. Use a large sharp knife to cut out 12-cm-wide strips. Cut each strip into 12-cm squares. Place a chocolate stick on each square and roll the dough over it, then add another stick and roll the dough over it too.
Arrange the pains au chocolat on a baking tray lined with baking parchment and leave to rise in a warm place for 1 hour. They should double in size.

BAKING
Preheat the oven to 180°C on the fan-assisted setting (or 200°C/Gas Mark 6).
In a bowl, beat the egg yolks with 2 tablespoons of water. Gently brush the pains au chocolat with this egg wash. Bake for 12 minutes, keeping a close eye on them to ensure they don't become too dark.

FOR THE LEAVENED LAMINATED DOUGH
500 g Italian '00' flour or plain flour

50 g caster sugar

10 g salt

120 g unsalted butter, softened

6 g active dried yeast

250 ml cold milk

250 g unsalted butter, chilled

FOR THE FILLING AND FINISHING
40 chocolate sticks

2 egg yolks

Makes about
20 pains au
chocolat

Preparation
time:
15 minutes

Cooking time:
12 minutes

Resting time:
4 hours

BRUNCH

PEPPER AND FETA LOAF

Preheat the oven to 180°C (Gas Mark 4).

In the mixer fitted with the pastry beater, add the flour, baking powder and salt, then mix on speed 1. Add the eggs, oil and milk, and increase to speed 2 for 2 minutes.

In the meantime, cut the peppers into small pieces and the cheese into cubes. Reduce the speed to 1 and add the peppers, cheese and herbes de Provence. When the batter is smooth, pour it into a loaf tin greased with oil.

Bake for 45 minutes. Turn out the loaf and leave to cool before slicing and serving.

150 g plain flour
11 g baking powder
½ tsp salt
3 eggs
100 ml olive oil
125 ml milk
150 g peppers marinated in olive oil
150 g feta cheese
1 tsp herbes de Provence

VARIATIONS

You can use sun-dried tomatoes instead of the marinated peppers. Instead of using fresh olive oil, you can use the marinating oil from the jar.

Makes
1 loaf
(Serves
10–12)

Preparation
time:
10 minutes

Cooking time:
45 minutes

CORNBREAD

In the mixer fitted with the dough hook, add the different flours. Add the salt and sugar to one side of the bowl and crumble in the yeast on the other side. Start the mixer on speed 1 and then add the water. Mix for 2 minutes on speed 1 until smooth, then increase to speed 2 and knead the dough for 7–8 minutes.

Lightly grease a bowl with oil. Shape the dough into a ball and put it into the bowl. Cover with a damp cloth and leave to rise at room temperature for 1 hour. The dough should double in size.

On a floured work surface, flatten the dough by folding and then shape it into a sausage the length of your loaf tin. Put it inside the tin. Cover with a cloth and leave to rise for 30 minutes–1 hour.

Preheat the oven to 200°C (Gas Mark 6). Place a container of water at the bottom of the oven.
Using a knife to score the top of the dough and lightly dust it with flour. Bake for 20–25 minutes. Turn out the cornbread and leave to cool.

250 g Italian '00' flour or plain flour
100 g maize flour (polenta/cornmeal)
7 g salt
5 g caster sugar
15 g fresh yeast (or 6 g active dried yeast)
240 ml lukewarm water
Oil

VARIATION

You can add sunflower seeds.

Makes
1 loaf
(Serves
10–12)

Preparation
time:
15 minutes

Cooking time:
20–25
minutes

Resting time:
1 hour
30 minutes–
2 hours

THREE-CHEESE SOUFFLÉS

Preheat the oven to 210°C (Gas Mark 6½). Separate the egg whites from the yolks. Grease 6 ramekins with butter and flour.

Melt the butter in a saucepan. Add the flour and mix briskly. Stir in the milk, a little at a time, until the mixture thickens. Remove from the heat, add the egg yolks and mix, then add the grated cheeses, salt and pepper.

Put the egg whites into the mixer fitted with the whisk and beat on speed 8 to stiff peaks. Gently fold the beaten egg whites into the previous mixture. Divide the mixture among the ramekins and bake for 15 minutes. Serve immediately.

4 eggs

50 g unsalted butter + a little for greasing

50 g plain flour

500 ml milk

40 g Cantal cheese

40 g aged mimolette cheese

40 g Emmental cheese

Salt

Pepper

VARIATIONS

You can add a little grated nutmeg. Vary the cheeses according to preference, including Parmesan, Comté, etc.

Serves 6

Preparation
time:
10 minutes

Cooking time:
15 minutes

HAM CROISSANTS

FOR THE LEAVENED LAMINATED DOUGH

Put the flour into the mixer fitted with the dough hook. Add the salt and sugar to one side of the bowl and crumble in the yeast on the other side. Run the mixer on speed 1 and then add 65 g of water and the milk. Add 25 g of the butter, cut into small pieces. Mix on speed 1 for 2 minutes, until smooth, then increase to speed 2 and knead the dough for 8–10 minutes.

Shape the dough into a ball and put it into a bowl. Cover with a damp cloth and leave to rise at room temperature for 1 hour. The dough should double in size.

On a floured work surface, flatten the dough to deflate it. Put the dough on a plate, cover with cling film and refrigerate for 1 hour.
Beat the remaining butter with a rolling pin to a roughly 10-cm square.
Roll out the dough into a 15-cm square. Place the butter square in the middle of the dough at a 45-degree angle, then cover with the dough as if making an envelope. The butter should be completely encased.

Roll out the dough lengthways to make a rectangle and make a double turn: fold the two shorter ends into the centre of the rectangle and then fold it in half like a book. Wrap the dough in cling film and rest for 30 minutes in the refrigerator. Roll it out again lengthways into a rectangle. Make a single turn: fold the dough in three. Wrap the dough in cling film and refrigerate again for 30 minutes.

Roll out the dough lengthways into a rectangle measuring about 20 x 60 cm. Cut out triangles with a 12-cm-wide base, top to bottom and bottom to top. Roll them up from the base to the tip, then arrange the croissants on a baking tray lined with baking parchment. Beat the egg and brush a little over the croissants. Leave the croissants to rise for 1 hour at room temperature.

Preheat the oven to 200°C (Gas Mark 6). Brush the croissants again with beaten egg. Bake for 15–20 minutes, until golden brown. Leave to cool.

FOR THE LEAVENED LAMINATED DOUGH
250 g Italian '00' flour or plain flour
5 g salt
5 g caster sugar
10 g fresh yeast
65 g milk
175 g unsalted butter
1 egg

FOR THE FILLING
2 ham slices
2 tbsp crème fraîche
30 g cheese, grated

Makes
8 croissants

Preparation
time:
45 minutes

Cooking time:
25–35
minutes

Resting time:
4 hours

FOR THE FILLING

Preheat the oven to 160°C (Gas Mark 3). Use a knife to cut an opening in each croissant. Spread a little crème fraîche inside each croissant and add a quarter slice of ham. Finish with a little grated cheese. Place the filled croissants on a baking tray lined with baking parchment and bake for 10–15 minutes. Serve hot.

SAVOURY SCONES

Beat the egg with the milk and add the salt. In the mixer fitted with the pastry beater, add the flour and butter. Mix on speed 1, gradually increasing it to speed 2, and beat for 3 minutes. Add the egg and milk mixture, then mix on speed 2 for 2 minutes.

Grate the cheese and roughly chop the tomato confit. Add them to the dough together with the herbes de Provence and mix on speed 1 for 1 minute. Leave the dough to rest for 30 minutes–1 hour.

On a floured work surface, roll out the dough to a thickness of 2.5 cm with a rolling pin. Cut out the scones using a biscuit cutter with a diameter of about 8 cm. Leave to rest for a further 30 minutes.

Preheat the oven to 180°C (Gas Mark 4). Brush the scones with the beaten egg yolk or milk, then bake for 15 minutes, until golden brown.

1 large egg
6 tbsp milk
½ tsp salt
300 g self-raising flour
100 g unsalted butter
200 g Cheddar cheese
50 g tomato confit
1 tbsp herbes de Provence
1 egg yolk or a little milk, for glazing

Serves 4

Preparation
time:
20 minutes

Cooking time:
15 minutes

Resting time:
1 hour–1 hour
30 minutes

CHEESE QUICHE

The previous day, make the pastry by putting all the ingredients together with 50 g of water into the mixer fitted with the dough hook and mixing on speed 1 to form a smooth ball of dough. Wrap in cling film and refrigerate overnight.

On the day, preheat the oven to 180°C (Gas Mark 4).

Roll out the pastry thinly with a rolling pin. Line a greased 17-cm-diameter and 8-cm-deep baking tin with the pastry. Cover with baking beans and bake for 10 minutes. Take out the weights and continue to bake for a further 5 minutes.

In the mixer fitted with the pastry beater, add all the ingredients for the filling. Mix on speed 1 for 3 minutes and then pour mixture into the pastry case. Bake for 30–35 minutes. The filling shouldn't be firmly set, only golden brown on top.

FOR THE PASTRY CASE
250 g strong bread flour

125 g unsalted butter, softened

4 g salt

FOR THE FILLING
4 eggs

125 g mascarpone cheese

100 g fromage frais

2 tbsp milk

150 g Cheddar cheese, grated

150 g bacon, cubed

1 tsp salt

1 tsp ground pepper

TIP Is there any leftover pastry? Freeze it for future use.

Serves 4

Preparation
time:
25 minutes

Cooking time:
50 minutes

Resting time:
overnight

SAVOURY SWEET POTATO PANCAKES

Boil the sweet potato for 15 minutes. Drain well.

In the mixer fitted with the pastry beater, mash the cooked sweet potato on speed 2 for 2 minutes to a smooth purée. Add the hazelnut milk, flour and maple syrup and mix on speed 1 to a very smooth paste.

Grease a non-stick frying pan well with oil and place over the heat. To make the pancakes, one at a time, add a small heap of the mixture to the pan. Wait for bubbles to form on the surface before turning it over over. Cook for a further 1 minute.

Serve the pancakes with the slices of smoked salmon, crème fraîche and lemon juice.

90 g sweet potato
250 ml hazelnut milk
150 g buckwheat or chestnut flour
2 tbsp maple syrup
A little vegetable oil (e.g. coconut oil)

FOR SERVING
A few slices of smoked salmon
A pot of quality crème fraîche
Juice of 1 lemon

Serves 4

Preparation
time:
15 minutes

Cooking time:
20 minutes

BRAZILIAN CHEESE BREADS

Grate the cheese. In a small saucepan, heat 90 ml of water with the milk, butter and salt.

Put the cassava starch into the mixer fitted with the pastry beater. Mix on speed 1 and pour in the hot butter-milk mixture. Add the egg, followed by the grated cheese. Mix on speed 2 for 2 minutes. Rest for 20 minutes.

Preheat the oven to 180°C (Gas Mark 4). Use your hands to shape the dough into small balls, the size of a ping-pong ball. Place on a baking tray lined with baking parchment. Bake for 25–30 minutes. Serve immediately.

125 g Beaufort or young Comté cheese
90 ml milk
65 g unsalted butter
½ tsp salt
250 g cassava (manioc) starch
1 small egg

TIPS

You can find a mix for making *pao de queijo*, often sold by the brand name Yoki, that only requires adding eggs and water.
You can vary the cheese by using Parmesan or Emmental cheese, among others.

Serves 4

Preparation
time:
20 minutes

Cooking time:
25–30
minutes

Resting time:
20 minutes

SALT BAGELS

FOR THE DOUGH
In a bowl, mix 60 ml of water with the yeast and sugar. Leave the mixture to foam for 5 minutes.

In the mixer fitted with the dough hook, add the flour and salt. Run the mixer on speed 1, then add the yeast and sugar mixture, oil and eggs. Knead on speed 1 for 2 minutes, then increase to speed 2 for 6 minutes.

RISING
Grease a bowl with 1 teaspoon of oil, turning the bowl to coat it well. Put the dough into the bowl. Cover with a cloth and leave to rise at room temperature for 30 minutes–1 hour, until the dough has almost doubled in size.

SHAPING
Knead the dough on a floured work surface. Shape it into a ball, then divide it into eight portions and shape each one into sausages about 12 cm long. Bring the two ends together and roll well to seal. Place the dough rings on a baking tray lined with baking parchment, cover with a clean cloth and leave to rest for 10 minutes.

BAKING AND FINISHING
Preheat the oven to 200°C (Gas Mark 6). Bring 7 litres of water to the boil and immerse the bagels, four at a time, for about 3 minutes, making sure to turn them over in the water. Drain, place on the baking tray and scatter over the coarse sea salt. Bake for about 30 minutes, depending on your oven and the size of the bagels. Turn them over and bake for a further 5 minutes, until golden brown. Leave to cool on a rack.

22 g active dried yeast
3 tbsp caster sugar
375 g bread flour
2 tsp fine salt
60 ml olive oil
2 eggs
Coarse sea salt

TIP These bagels can be stored frozen.

Makes
8 bagels
(10 cm in
diameter)

Preparation
time:
30 minutes

Cooking time:
40 minutes

Resting time:
40 minutes–
1 hour
10 minutes

PESTO BREAD

FOR THE DOUGH

Mix the water with the sugar and yeast in a bowl. Leave to foam for 10 minutes.

In the mixer fitted with the paddle attachment, add the flour, ground almonds, guar gum and salt, and mix on speed 1. Add the water-yeast mixture and 1 tablespoon of the pesto, then knead on speed 2 for 3 minutes, until smooth.

SHAPING

Cover the work surface with baking parchment and generously dust with flour. Dust your hands and the dough well with flour, and shape the dough into a ball. Flatten it into a rectangle measuring about 30 x 20 cm. Spread the remaining pesto over the entire surface of the dough, then roll it up like a scroll.

RISING

Arrange the dough in a 20-cm-diameter round baking tin lined with baking parchment. Cover with a damp cloth and leave to rise in a warm place for 1 hour.

BAKING

Preheat the oven to 200°C (Gas Mark 6). Brush the bread with olive oil and scatter over the chopped pine nuts. Bake for 25 minutes. Leave to cool before slicing.

250 ml lukewarm water

1 tsp cane sugar

5 g active dried yeast

220 g gluten-free bread flour

30 g ground almonds

1 tsp guar gum

1 tbsp salt

4 tbsp pesto

1 tbsp olive oil

1 tbsp pine nuts, chopped

TIP

To make your own pesto, blend 1 bunch of basil with 2 tablespoons each of almonds, olive oil and water along with the juice of half a lemon and half a clove of garlic. Season with salt and pepper.

POTATO BREAD

FOR THE POTATOES

Peel and dice the potatoes. This should make 200 g. Put them into a saucepan of cold salted water and bring to the boil. Cook for about 10 minutes, until tender. Drain the potatoes, collecting the cooking water, then mash with 1 tablespoon of olive oil.

Add 150 ml of the cooking water to a bowl together with the sugar and yeast. Leave to foam for 10 minutes.

FOR THE DOUGH

In the mixer fitted with the pastry beater, combine the flour, salt and herbes de Provence, then add the mashed potato. Pour the water-yeast mixture into the bowl and mix for a few minutes, until smooth and very sticky. Add a little water if necessary. Put the dough into a loaf tin lined with baking parchment. Cover with a damp cloth and leave to rise in a warm place for 1 hour.

BAKING

Preheat the oven to 180°C (Gas Mark 4).
Brush the dough with olive oil and bake for 45 minutes. Leave to cool before serving.

250 g potatoes
2 tbsp olive oil
1 pinch cane sugar
5 g fresh yeast
250 g gluten-free bread flour
1 tsp salt
1 tbsp herbes de Provence

TIP

You can cut thin slices from the potato bread and spread with tapenade to have as a snack.

Makes 1 loaf

Preparation
time:
20 minutes

Cooking time:
1 hour
10 minutes

Resting time:
1 hour
10 minutes

GLUTEN-FREE COURGETTE AND RICOTTA
BLINIS

FOR THE BLINI MIX
Wash, top and tail, and grate the courgettes. In the mixer fitted with the paddle attachment, mix the eggs, cornflour, ricotta, salt and pepper on speed 4 for 2 minutes. Add the grated courgettes and mix on speed 2 for 1 minute.

FOR THE BLINIS
Lightly oil a frying pan, then add small heaps of blini mixture, spacing them well apart. After a few minutes, check to see if the undersides are done, and if so, turn them over. Transfer the cooked blinis to a plate and repeat until you have used all the mixture.

Spread a little ricotta over each blini and scatter over with chopped chives and a little grated lemon zest. Serve immediately.

FOR THE BLINIS
2 courgettes
2 eggs
2 tbsp cornflour
150 g ricotta cheese
Salt
Pepper

TOPPING
100 g ricotta cheese
Chives
Zest of 1 lemon

VARIATION

If you wish, you can add a little salmon roe to the ricotta topping.

Serves 4

Preparation
time:
10 minutes

Cooking time:
10 minutes

AVOCADO TOASTS

FOR THE MASHED AVOCADO
2 ripe avocados
1 lemon
⅓ bunch fresh coriander
1 tbsp olive oil
1 tbsp fresh harissa
4 thick slices of fresh bread (charcoal bread, pain de campagne, seeded multigrain bread, etc.)

TOPPINGS

FOR THE ROASTED SWEET POTATO
1 sweet potato (about 300 g)
Olive oil
200 g feta cheese
Fleur de sel

FOR THE ROASTED CHERRY TOMATOES
250 g cherry tomatoes
1 tbsp caster sugar
1 tsp fine salt
3 tbsp olive oil
1 sprig fresh thyme

FOR THE RAW COURGETTE RIBBONS
1 courgette (about 200 g)
Juice of ½ lemon
2 tbsp olive oil
Fleur de sel

FOR THE SAUTÉED MUSHROOMS
1 small shallot
400 g assorted mushrooms (chanterelles, button mushrooms, oyster mushrooms)
20 g salted butter
Blueberries

FOR THE POACHED EGG
1 egg per person
1 roll of cling film
Olive oil

FOR THE CRISPY SMOKED STREAKY BACON
2 slices of smoked streaky bacon per person

Serves 4

Preparation
time:
10 minutes

Cooking time:
up to
20 minutes,
depending on
the topping

FOR THE MASHED AVOCADO

Wash the lemon, grate the zest and squeeze the juice. Wash, dry and finely chop the coriander.

Halve and scoop out the flesh from the avocados. Put the flesh into the mixer fitted with the pastry beater. Mix on speed 1 for 2 minutes. Immediately add the lemon juice, grated lemon zest, olive oil, fresh harissa and coriander. Mix on speed 1 for 1 minute.

Spread the mashed avocado generously over the slices of bread, freshly toasted. Combine the avocado base with the topping(s) of your choice.

TOPPINGS

FOR THE ROASTED SWEET POTATO

Preheat the oven to 180°C (Gas Mark 4). Peel and dice the sweet potato. Drizzle with a little olive oil and mix well. Spread the diced sweet potato out over a baking tray lined with baking parchment and crumble the feta cheese over the top. Bake for 20 minutes with the oven rack in the middle position, stirring once halfway through. Sprinkle the freshly roasted sweet potato with fleur de sel.

FOR THE ROASTED CHERRY TOMATOES

Preheat the oven to 180°C (Gas Mark 4). Wash and halve the tomatoes. In a bowl, mix the sugar with the salt, olive oil and crumbled thyme. Add the tomatoes and mix well. Spread the tomatoes, spaced well apart, over a baking tray lined with baking parchment and roast for 15 minutes.

FOR THE RAW COURGETTE RIBBONS

Wash and cut the courgette into thin ribbons using a vegetable peeler, paring knife or a mandoline. Drizzle with lemon juice and olive oil and scatter over the fleur de sel. Gently mix everything together.

FOR THE SAUTÉED MUSHROOMS

Peel and finely chop the shallot. Wash all the mushrooms and slice the button mushrooms. Melt the butter in a frying pan and sauté the shallot for 2 minutes, to soften. Then add the mushrooms and sauté over a high heat for 4 minutes, stirring once or twice at most. Spread the sautéed mushrooms on the toast, then scatter with the blueberries.

FOR THE POACHED EGG

Bring a large amount of water to the boil in a saucepan. Line a small bowl with cling film and brush lightly with the oil. Crack the egg into the bowl and seal the cling film by tying a knot. Immerse in the simmering water for 4 minutes.

FOR THE CRISPY SMOKED STREAKY BACON

Preheat the oven to 180°C (Gas Mark 4). Spread the bacon over a baking tray, spaced slightly apart. Cook in the oven for 5–6 minutes, keeping a close eye on it.

SUMMER VEGETABLE TART

FOR THE PUFF PASTRY
Make the puff pastry as described on p. 17.

Preheat the oven to 180°C (Gas Mark 4).

On baking parchment, roll out the pastry into a large disc with a diameter of about 40 cm. You can decorate the edges if you wish.

FOR THE TOPPING
In the mixer fitted with the pastry beater, mix the ricotta cheese, mustard and olive oil. Season with salt and pepper. Spread this mixture over the pastry, making sure to leave a border all around the edge of the tart.

Wash, top and tail, and halve the courgettes length-ways. Thinly slice using a mandoline or knife. Distribute the slices over the tart. Add a few cherry tomatoes, cut into quarters. Wash and chop the basil, then scatter over the tart. Season with salt and pepper. Bake for 35–40 minutes. The edges of the tart should be golden brown.

FOR THE PUFF PASTRY
250 g Italian '00' flour or plain flour
200 g unsalted butter
5 g salt
120 ml water

FOR THE TOPPING
4 tbsp ricotta cheese
1 tbsp wholegrain mustard
1 tbsp olive oil
3 courgettes
Cherry tomatoes
Basil leaves
Salt
Pepper

VARIATIONS

Instead of the ricotta cheese, you can use fresh goat's cheese or even tapenade or pesto. For a gluten-free version, replace the wheat flour with 150 g rice flour and 50 g cornflour.

Serves 6

Preparation
time:
10 minutes

Cooking time:
35–40
minutes

Resting time:
30 minutes

LEMON AND HADDOCK GOUGÈRES

FOR THE CHOUX PASTRY
Preheat the oven to 170°C (Gas Mark 3½).
Make the choux pastry as described on p. 14 using the ingredients and quantities given here.
Put the pastry into a piping bag fitted with a 10-mm plain round nozzle. On a baking tray lined with baking parchment, pipe 4–5-cm-diameter choux buns. Bake for about 25 minutes. Leave to cool.

FOR THE FILLING
In the mixer fitted with the whisk, pour in the cream with the mascarpone. Whisk on speed 8 until smooth. Zest and squeeze the lemon. Cut the fish into very small cubes. When the cream is whipped, add the lemon juice and zest, season with a little salt and pepper, then fold in gently with a rubber palette knife. Finally, fold in the fish. Transfer to a piping bag fitted with a star nozzle. Cut the tops off the choux buns and pipe full of the cream filling. Refrigerate until ready to serve.

FOR THE CHOUX PASTRY
130 g water
55 g unsalted butter
1 pinch salt
1 pinch sugar
80 g plain flour
2 eggs

FOR THE FILLING
115 g whipping cream
50 g mascarpone cheese
1 organic lemon
1 small fillet smoked haddock
Salt
Pepper

VARIATION

You can replace the haddock with smoked salmon and add a little dill.

Makes
10 gougères

Preparation
time:
15 minutes

Cooking time:
25 minutes

QUICHE LORRAINE

or

FOR THE SHORTCRUST PASTRY
Make the pastry as described on p. 16.

FOR THE QUICHE
Preheat the oven to 180°C on the fan-assisted setting (or 200°C/Gas Mark 6).

Thinly slice the bacon. Quickly sauté the bacon in a frying pan without drying it out. Pour off any excess fat.

In the mixer fitted with the pastry beater, add the eggs, crème fraîche, milk and spices. Beat on speed 2 for 1 minute, then increase to speed 4 for 1 minute. Add the bacon and grated cheese, reduce to speed 2 and mix for 1 minute. Season with salt and pepper.

Roll out the pastry to a thickness of about 3 mm, then line a 20-cm-diameter tart tin or stainless steel ring. Prick the pastry case with a fork and fill the quiche mixture.

Bake for about 35 minutes.

FOR THE SHORTCRUST PASTRY
200 g plain flour
100 g unsalted butter
2 g salt
35 g lukewarm water

FOR THE QUICHE FILLING
200 g smoked bacon
4 eggs
150 g crème fraîche
220 g semi-skimmed milk
1 tsp grated nutmeg
1 pinch cayenne pepper
100 g Gruyère or Comté cheese, grated
Salt
Pepper

VARIATIONS

For a meat-free quiche that still has a lovely smoky flavour, use smoked tofu; you can also replace the bacon with smoked salmon.
If you want to reduce the saltiness of the bacon, blanch it in boiling water for 30 seconds.
For a lighter version, you can use leek fondue instead of the bacon and cheese.

Serves 6–8
(makes 1
tart/
20 cm in
diameter)

Preparation
time:
20 minutes

Cooking time:
35 minutes

RASPBERRY AND WHITE CHOCOLATE
CUPCAKES

The previous day, make the raspberry jam and the white chocolate whipped ganache icing.

FOR THE RASPBERRY JAM
Wash and hull the strawberries. In the mixer fitted with the pastry beater, add the fruits and sugar. Mix on speed 2 for 2 minutes. Transfer the mixture to a saucepan and cook over a high heat for about 15 minutes. Pour into a jar.

FOR THE WHIPPED WHITE CHOCOLATE GANACHE
Melt the white chocolate and put it into a mixing bowl. Heat 60 g of the cream with the vanilla extract. Pour the cream over the melted chocolate, a third at a time, mixing well each time with a palette knife. Add the remaining cold cream and mix well. Cover with cling film in direct contact and set aside overnight in the refrigerator.

FOR THE CUPCAKES
Preheat the oven to 180°C (Gas Mark 4). In the mixer fitted with the whisk, add the sugar, eggs and vanilla extract. Run the mixer on speed 1, gradually increasing it to speed 8, then whisk on speed 8 for 5 minutes, until the mixture doubles in volume. Replace the whisk with the flex edge beater. Mix on speed 1, then add the flour, baking powder and salt. Melt the butter and mix well with the batter until smooth. Divide the batter into cupcake moulds, filling halfway. Bake for 15 minutes.

ASSEMBLY
Scoop out the centre of the cupcakes with a spoon and fill with raspberry jam. Put the white chocolate ganache into the mixer fitted with the whisk. Whisk on speed 8 to the consistency of whipped cream. Transfer the ganache to a piping bag fitted with a star nozzle and ice the cupcakes. Decorate according to preference.

FOR THE RASPBERRY JAM (FOR 1 JAR)
80 g strawberries
200 g raspberries
200 g caster sugar

FOR THE WHITE CHOCOLATE WHIPPED GANACHE ICING
50 g white chocolate
180 g whipping cream
1 tsp vanilla extract

FOR THE CUPCAKES
75 g caster sugar
2 eggs
1 tsp vanilla extract
90 g plain flour
1 level tsp baking powder
1 pinch salt
75 g unsalted butter

Makes
8 cupcakes

Preparation
time:
25 minutes

Cooking time:
30 minutes

Resting time:
Overnight

AFTERNOON TEA

KUGELHOPF

FOR THE DOUGH
In a saucepan, cover the raisins with water and bring to the boil for 2 minutes to swell. Drain and leave to cool. In the mixer fitted with the dough hook, add the eggs with the cold milk. Crumble the yeast over the eggs and milk for better distribution. Add the flour, sugar and salt. Knead on speed 1 for 5 minutes, then increase to speed 2 and knead for 6–8 minutes.
When the dough pulls away from sides of the bowl and forms a ball, add the softened butter, cut into small cubes. Knead the dough on speed 2 for 6–8 minutes, until the butter is incorporated and the dough comes away from the bowl in a smooth ball.
Add the cold swollen raisins to the dough. Knead until smooth.

RISING
Take the dough out of the mixer and shape into a ball. Place in a bowl and cover with cling film in direct contact. Leave to rise at room temperature for 1 hour.
Deflate the dough, shape it into a ball and wrap in cling film. Refrigerate for 3 hours.

FOR THE KUGELHOPF
Chill the kugelhopf mould in the freezer for 10 minutes. Brush the inside of the very cold mould with melted butter and line the sides with flaked almonds.
Deflate and then shape the dough into a ball. Use your forefinger to make a hole in the centre of the dough. Shape the dough into a ring. Put the dough ring into the mould and press it down into the base of the mould with your knuckles to prevent the formation of air bubbles.

PROVING
Place the mould on the oven baking tray and prove in an improvised proving oven at 24°C for 2 hours (see p. 24).

BAKING AND FINISHING
Take the kugelhopf out of the oven. Preheat the oven to 180°C (Gas Mark 4) with the baking tray inside. Place the mould on the hot baking tray and bake at 170°C (Gas Mark 3½) for 30-35 minutes. Take the kugelhopf out of the oven and turn it out of the mould while still hot. Return it to the baking tray in the oven, without the mould, and bake for a further 10 minutes. Transfer to a rack and dust with icing sugar. Serve warm or cold.

FOR THE BRIOCHE DOUGH
100 g raisins

90 g (2 small) eggs

135 g milk

17 g fresh yeast

335 g Italian '00' flour or plain flour

34 g caster sugar

7 g fine salt

90 g unsalted butter, softened

FINISHING
Flaked almonds

Icing sugar

TIP

If you wish to extend the shelf life of your kugelhopf, you can soak it with a light vanilla syrup when it comes out of the oven.

Makes 1 large
kugelhopf

Preparation
time:
45 minutes

Cooking time:
45 minutes

Resting time:
6 hours
10 minutes

BANANA BREAD

FOR THE BATTER
Preheat the oven to 180°C (Gas Mark 4).
Peel and slice the bananas. Put the slices into the mixer fitted with the flex edge beater, and purée on speed 2 for 1 minute. Melt the butter. Increase the speed to 4 and add the brown sugar and eggs, followed by the melted butter. Add the flour and baking powder all at once and beat for 2 minutes. Reduce the speed to 1, add the chocolate chips and mix for 30 seconds.

BAKING AND FINISHING
Grease a loaf tin with butter and flour and pour in the mixture. Peel and cut the remaining banana lengthways. Arrange the halves on top of the mixture and scatter over the vanilla sugar. Bake for 1 hour. Leave to cool before turning out.

2 large ripe bananas +
1 for decoration
130 g unsalted butter
100 g brown sugar
2 eggs
250 g Italian '00' flour
or plain flour
11 g baking powder
120 g chocolate chips
8 g vanilla sugar

TIPS
Make sure you use very ripe bananas for this recipe. You can vary the recipe by using caramel chips.

Serves 8

Preparation time: 10 minutes

Cooking time: 1 hour

CARROT CUPCAKES

FOR THE CUPCAKES

Preheat the oven to 160°C (Gas Mark 3).
In the mixer fitted with the pastry beater, add the sugar, oil and eggs, and mix on speed 1 for 2 minutes. Add the flour, baking powder and spices, then mix on speed 1 for 1 minute. Grate the zest of the whole orange and squeeze it for the juice. Incorporate the orange juice and zest into the mixture, followed by the carrots and nuts. Mix until smooth.

Divide the mixture into 8–10 holes of a cupcake mould greased with butter and bake for 12 minutes. Allow the cupcakes to rest for a few minutes before turning out and leaving to cool on a rack.

FOR THE ICING

In the meantime, make the icing by mixing the orange juice with the icing sugar. The icing should be quite thick with a consistency similar to that of crème fraîche. Use a palette knife to spread the icing over the cupcakes and scatter them with chopped walnuts.

FOR THE CUPCAKES

150 g raw sugar

100 ml sunflower or rapeseed oil

2 eggs

220 g plain flour

11 g baking powder

2 tsp cinnamon

½ tsp grated nutmeg

1 untreated orange

300 g carrots, grated

50 g walnuts, roughly chopped

FOR THE ICING

Juice of ½ orange

200 g icing sugar

50 g walnuts, roughly chopped

TIP

You can also make one large cake and bake it for 30 minutes in a 22-cm-diameter round cake tin.

Makes 8–10
cupcakes

Preparation
time:
15 minutes

Cooking time:
12 minutes

FLAKY BRIOCHE
WITH A RUNNY CHOCOLATE CENTRE

FOR THE CHOCOLATE CENTRES

The previous day, melt the chocolate over a bain-marie. In a bowl, whisk together the cream, honey and cornflour. Transfer the mixture to a saucepan and bring to the boil for 1–2 minutes. Pour the mixture over the melted chocolate at 55°C and whisk until smooth.
Pour the mixture into small cylindrical moulds and freeze.

FOR THE DOUGH

Using the ingredients given here, except for the dry butter and beaten egg, make the brioche dough as described on p. 14.

RISING

Take the dough out of the mixer and shape into a ball. Place in a bowl and cover with cling film in direct contact. Leave to rise at room temperature for 2 hours. Deflate the dough and then shape it into a ball. Wrap the dough with cling film. Refrigerate for 12 hours.

TURNING (FOLDING)

On the actual day, weigh out the dry butter and lightly pound it with a rolling pin until it has the same consistency as the dough. Shape it into a square, wrap with cling film and refrigerate.
Deflate the dough with the palm of your hand. With a rolling pin, roll out the dough into a square. Place the square of butter in the middle of the dough at a 45-degree angle. Encase the butter in the dough.
Roll out the dough into a rectangle the length of the rolling pin. Then fold it in three. Roll out the dough into a rectangle again, then fold in three again. Wrap the dough with cling film and refrigerate.

SHAPING

Roll out the dough into a rectangle measuring about 60 x 20 cm. Divide it into three strips, each about 6 cm wide. Turn out the frozen chocolate centres, lay them on the pastry strips and roll them up. Place each brioche in the middle of a cake ring greased with butter placed on baking parchment.

PROVING

Prove the brioches in an improvised proving oven at 24°C for 2 hours (see p. 24).

FOR THE CHOCOLATE CENTRES

125 g dark couverture chocolate

115 g whipping cream

10 g acacia honey

6 g cornflour

FOR THE BRIOCHE DOUGH

130 g (3 small) eggs

50 g water

10 g active dried yeast

330 g Italian '00' flour or plain flour

40 g caster sugar

6 g fine salt

70 g unsalted butter

100 g dry butter

1 beaten egg, for glazing

FINISHING

Icing sugar

TIP

If you don't have small cylindrical moulds for the chocolate centres, you can use an ice cube tray.

BAKING AND FINISHING

Take the brioches out of the oven and rest at room temperature for 10 minutes. Preheat the oven to 180°C (Gas Mark 4) with the oven baking tray inside. Place the brioches on the hot baking tray and bake at 170°C (Gas Mark 3½) for 30–35 minutes.

Transfer to a rack. When cold, sprinkle the brioches with icing sugar.

SUNDAES
WITH DULCE
DE LECHE

FOR THE YOGHURT ICE CREAM
In the mixer fitted with the whisk, whisk the egg whites with the salt and lemon juice on speed 8. When the egg whites become foamy, add the caster sugar while continuing to whisk. Then add the icing sugar and whisk to stiff peaks. Gently fold in the yoghurt. Transfer the mixture to a stainless steel container and freeze for 3 hours, stirring every 35 minutes. Do not leave the ice cream in the freezer for more than 5 hours.

FOR THE TOPPING
Slice the bananas, chop up the chocolate, melt the dulce de leche and toast the roughly chopped hazelnuts. Spoon the yoghurt ice cream into bowls, drizzle with dulce de leche and top with the bananas, chocolate and hazelnuts.

FOR THE YOGHURT ICE CREAM
2 egg whites
1 pinch salt
1 tsp lemon juice
30 g caster sugar
30 g icing sugar
500 g Greek yoghurt

FOR THE TOPPING
2 bananas
50 g dark chocolate
4 tbsp dulce de leche (caramel spread)
50 g hazelnuts

TIP

The sundaes should be made on the day they are to be consumed so that there is no need to freeze the ice cream for more than 5 hours. If you want to store the yoghurt ice cream, it should be churned in an ice cream maker.

Serves 4

Preparation
time:
30 minutes

Resting time:
3 hours

MATCHA AND PISTACHIO FINANCIERS

Preheat the oven to 160°C on the fan-assisted setting (or 180°C/Gas Mark 4).
In a small saucepan, melt the butter over a low heat until it turns a nice golden colour. Use a fine sieve to filter out the browned milk solids, then leave to cool.

Sift the flour and matcha together. In the mixer fitted with the pastry beater, mix the sifted powders, icing sugar and ground almonds on speed 1. Mix in the egg whites and then the melted butter on speed 1 for 2 minutes. Increase to speed 2 for 2 minutes, until the mixture is smooth.

Transfer the mixture to a piping bag with a plain nozzle, then fill the cavities of a silicone financier mould. Decorate the top with chopped pistachio pieces and bake for 8–10 minutes. Take out the financiers as soon as they start to turn golden and wait for a few minutes before turning them out. Leave to cool on a rack.

70 g unsalted butter
50 g plain flour
1½ tsp matcha powder, culinary grade
150 g icing sugar
80 g ground almonds
4 small egg whites
40 g pistachios, chopped

TIP

The financiers will become even firmer as they cool, so take care not to bake them for too long.

APPLE AND PEAR CRUMBLE

Preheat the oven to 180°C (Gas Mark 4).
Peel and thinly slice the fruit. Grease a dish measuring about 20 x 30 cm with butter and sprinkle with sugar. Arrange the fruit slices inside.

In the mixer fitted with the pastry beater, mix the flour, ground almonds, brown sugar, butter and vanilla powder on speed 4 for 2 minutes. Cover the fruit with the dough, crumbling it through your fingertips. Bake for 30 minutes. Serve warm or cold with cream or vanilla ice cream.

5 apples
3 pears
150 g plain flour
125 g ground almonds
150 g brown sugar
200 g semi-salted butter
1 tsp vanilla powder

VARIATIONS

Substitute ground hazelnuts for the ground almonds and add chopped hazelnuts. You can also add spices to the mixture such as cinnamon, ginger and tonka bean. Vary the fruits according to the season.

SERVES 4–6

Preparation
time:
10 minutes

Cooking time:
30 minutes

APPLE KUCHEN

FOR THE BRIOCHE DOUGH
125 g raisins
50 g dark agricultural rum
Zest of ½ lemon
80 g full-fat milk
2 vanilla pods
50 g (1) egg
25 g (1 large) egg yolk
8 g fresh yeast
285 g Italian '00' flour or plain flour
50 g brown beet sugar
6 g fine salt
126 g unsalted butter

FOR THE BUTTERKUCHEN PASTE
165 g almond paste (50% almonds)
Zest of 1 lemon
165 g unsalted butter, softened

FOR THE CARAMELISED APPLES
4 Granny Smith apples
45 g unsalted butter
45 g brown sugar
1 vanilla pod
Zest of 1 lemon

FOR THE CRUMBLE TOPPING
160 g Italian '00' flour or plain flour
120 g brown sugar
1 g cinnamon
1 pinch salt
1 g baking powder
115 g unsalted butter, softened

Makes
2 medium
kuchen

Preparation
time:
1 hour
20 minutes

Cooking
time: 15–20
minutes

Resting time:
3 hours

APPLE
KUCHEN

FOR THE DOUGH
Make the dough as described on p. 14.

RISING
Take the dough out of the mixer and shape into a ball.
Place in a bowl and cover with cling film in direct con-
tact. Leave to rise at room temperature for 2 hours.

FOR THE BUTTERKUCHEN PASTE
In the mixer fitted with the paddle attachment, beat
the almond paste with the lemon zest until creamy.
Gradually add the softened butter, cut into small cubes.
Beat the paste to the consistency of a smooth cream.
Set aside in a bowl covered with cling film in direct
contact at room temperature.

FOR THE CARAMELISED APPLES
Peel, core and cut the apples into thin wedges. In a
frying pan, melt the butter, add the sugar, split and
scraped vanilla pod and the grated lemon zest. Add the
apple wedges to the pan and caramelise on both sides.
Transfer to kitchen paper and leave to cool to room
temperature.

FOR THE CRUMBLE TOPPING
In the mixer fitted with the pastry beater, add the flour,
sugar, cinnamon, salt, baking powder and softened butter, cut into small cubes. Beat on speed 1 to a crumbly
consistency. Transfer to a container and refrigerate.

FOR THE KUCHEN
Deflate the brioche dough and divide it into two 400-g
portions. Using a rolling pin, roll out each piece into a
20-cm square.
Grease two baking frames with butter and place them
on baking parchment. Lay the dough squares in the
middle of the frames and flatten them with the back
of your hand until they extend to the corners of the
frames.

TIP

If you have one, use a
size 13 plain nozzle to
pipe the butterkuchen
paste balls.

PROVING

Prove the brioches in an improvised proving oven at 24°C for 1 hour (see p. 24).

ASSEMBLY AND BAKING

Arrange the caramelised apple wedges over the entire surface of the brioche squares. Fill a piping bag with the butterkuchen and pipe randomly placed balls of paste spaced apart over the surface of the brioches. Scatter over the crumble topping.

Preheat the oven to 170°C (Gas Mark 3½) with the oven baking tray inside. Place the brioches on the hot baking tray and bake at 165°C (Gas Mark 3) for 15–20 minutes. Carefully transfer the brioches in their frames to a rack. When the brioches are completely cold, use a small knife to release their frames and unmould.

CARAMEL BRIOCHE
WITH CARAMELISED HAZELNUTS

FOR THE DOUGH
Make the brioche dough as described on p. 14.

RISING
Take the dough out of the mixer and shape it into a ball. Place it in a bowl and cover with cling film in direct contact. Leave to rise at room temperature for 1 hour. Deflate and then shape the dough into a ball. Wrap the dough with cling film. Refrigerate for 2 hours.

FOR THE PASTRY CREAM
Combine the milk, melted butter, seeds from the split and scraped vanilla pods and half the sugar in a saucepan over the heat.
In a bowl, blanch the egg yolks by whisking them with the remaining sugar until thick and pale. Mix in the cornflour.
When the milk comes to the boil, mix a small amount into the blanched egg yolks.
Return the mixture to the pan and cook for 4 minutes over a low heat while continuing to stir. Transfer the pastry cream to a dish, cover with cling film in direct contact and chill in the freezer for 15–20 minutes. Set aside in the refrigerator.

FOR THE CARAMEL CREAM
Soften the gelatine leaves in a bowl of cold water. In a saucepan, cook the sugar to a dry caramel.
In another saucepan, combine the cream, glucose and seeds from the split and scraped vanilla pods, and bring to the boil. Add this mixture to the caramel.
Remove from heat and add the egg yolks while whisking briskly. Squeeze and mix in the gelatine, transfer to a piping bag and leave to cool to room temperature.

SHAPING
Deflate the dough and roll it out into a rectangle with a rolling pin. Brush the edges of the dough with a little beaten egg.
Whisk the pastry cream until smooth and then spread it over the dough. Pipe horizontal lines of caramel cream over the pastry cream. Scatter with the chopped caramelised hazelnuts.

FOR THE BRIOCHE DOUGH
200 g (4) eggs
15 g fresh yeast
330 g Italian '00' flour or plain flour
60 g caster sugar
7 g fine salt
170 g unsalted butter
1 beaten egg, for glazing

FOR THE PASTRY CREAM
250 g full-fat milk
50 g unsalted butter, melted
2 vanilla pods
25 g caster sugar
50 g (2 large) egg yolks
23 g cornflour

FOR THE CARAMEL CREAM
2 gelatine leaves (4 g)
130 g caster sugar
220 g whipping cream
20 g glucose syrup
4 vanilla pods
50 g (2 large) egg yolks

FINISHING
Liquid caramel
Caramelised hazelnuts

TIP

If you have one, you can use a size 10 plain nozzle to pipe the caramel cream.

**Makes
10 individual
brioches**

**Preparation
time:
1 hour
10 minutes**

**Cooking time:
25 minutes**

**Resting time:
5 hours
30 minutes**

Gently roll up the dough and chill in the freezer for 15 minutes to make it easier to cut.
Use a knife to cut the slightly frozen dough into 1.5-cm thick discs. Lay them on baking parchment.
Brush the tops of the brioches with beaten egg.

PROVING
Prove the brioches in an improvised proving oven at 24°C for 2 hours (see p. 24).

BAKING AND FINISHING
Take the brioches out of the oven and rest at room temperature for 10 minutes. Preheat the oven to 180°C (Gas Mark 4) with the oven baking tray inside. Glaze the brioches again. Place the brioches on the hot baking tray and bake at 170°C (Gas Mark 3½) for 15–18 minutes.
Transfer to a rack. Decorate with liquid caramel and caramelised hazelnuts.

CINNAMON ROLLS
(KANELBULLAR)

FOR THE DOUGH

Make the brioche dough as described on p. 14 using the quantities given here. After kneading, rest the dough for 45 minutes–1 hour at room temperature, in which time the flavour of the dough will develop.

FOR THE FILLING

Soften the butter by stirring until creamy. Add the sugar, salt and cinnamon.

FOR THE ROLLS

Roll out the brioche dough into a rectangle of roughly 20 x 30 cm. Spread the filling evenly over the top, leaving a 1-cm border of dough around the edge. Fold into thirds, letter style, then use a rolling pin to roll back out into a 20 x 30-cm rectangle. Cut lengthways into 12 strips, each about 3.3 cm wide.

Turn each strip to make a twist, then roll up each twist. Glaze the rolls with the beaten egg. Prove the rolls in a warm place (such as inside a cold oven heated with a bowl of hot water) at a temperature of 25–30°C for about 1 hour 45 minutes.

Preheat the oven to 180°C (Gas Mark 4). Glaze the rolls again with the beaten egg. Bake for 18 minutes. Leave to cool on a rack.

FOR THE BRIOCHE DOUGH

250 g Italian '00' flour or plain flour

25 g sugar

5 g salt

15 g fresh yeast

150 g (3) eggs, cold

100 g unsalted butter

FOR THE FILLING

60 g unsalted butter

80 g brown sugar or raw sugar

1 pinch salt

4 tsp cinnamon

GLAZING

1 egg

VARIATION

Scandinavians love this brioche roll! You can use cardamom instead of cinnamon for the filling.

Makes 12 rolls

Preparation
time:
25 minutes

Cooking time:
18 minutes

Resting time:
2 hours
45 minutes

PANETTONE

FOR THE DOUGH
The previous day, soak the sultanas in the rum for 12 hours.

On the actual day, put the eggs, honey and milk into the mixer fitted with the dough hook. Crumble the yeast over the mixture for better distribution. Add the seeds from the split and scraped vanilla pod. Add the flour, salt and sugar. Knead on speed 1 for 5 minutes, then increase to speed 4 for 6 minutes.
When the dough pulls away from sides of the bowl and forms a ball, mix in the softened butter, cut into small cubes on speed 1.
Knead the dough on speed 2 for 3 minutes, then increase to speed 4 for 3 minutes, until the butter is incorporated and the dough pulls away from the sides of the bowl in a smooth ball.
Drain the rum-soaked sultanas and mix them into the dough on speed 1 together with the candied orange peel, cut into small dice. Knead until the peel is evenly distributed through the dough.

RISING
Take the dough out of the mixer and shape into a ball. Place in a bowl and cover with cling film in direct contact. Leave to rise at room temperature for 1 hour.
Deflate the dough and then shape it into a ball. Wrap the dough in cling film. Refrigerate for 2 hours.

FOR THE ALMOND GLAZE
Mix the caster sugar with the egg whites. Gently mix in the almonds. Cover the mixture with cling film in direct contact and set aside at room temperature.

SHAPING
Divide and weigh out the dough into two 390-g portions, then shape them into balls. Grease cake rings with butter and line with a strip of baking parchment. Place the rings on baking parchment. Put the dough balls into the centre of the cake rings and flatten with the back of your hand.

PROVING
Prove the brioches in an improvised proving oven at 24°C for 2 hours (see p. 24).

FOR THE BRIOCHE DOUGH
83 g sultanas

90 g of white agricultural rum

163 g (3 large) eggs

13 g honey

13 g full-fat milk

13 g fresh yeast

1 vanilla pod

250 g Italian '00' flour or plain flour

7 g fine salt

13 g caster sugar

150 g unsalted butter, softened

83 g candied orange peel

FOR THE ALMOND GLAZE
35 g caster sugar

90 g (3) egg whites

90 g flaked almonds

Makes
2 medium
panettoni

Preparation
time:
45 minutes

Cooking time:
35–40
minutes

Resting time:
5 hours

ASSEMBLY AND BAKING

Take the brioches out of the oven and rest at room temperature for 10 minutes. Preheat the oven to 180°C (Gas Mark 4) with the oven baking tray inside.

Use a spoon to spread the almond glaze over the brioches. Place the brioches on the hot baking tray and bake at 170°C (Gas Mark 3½) for 35–40 minutes.

Slide the panettoni in their rings onto a rack. Take them out of their rings while still warm and leave to cool.

BRIOCHE ROYALE

FOR THE DOUGH

In the mixer fitted with the dough hook, add half the eggs with the cold milk. Crumble the yeast over the eggs and milk for better distribution. Add the flour, sugar and salt. Knead on speed 1 for 5 minutes, then increase to speed 2 for 3 minutes, gradually adding the remaining eggs.

When the dough pulls away from sides of the bowl and forms a ball, mix in the softened butter, cut into small cubes, on speed 1. Knead the dough on speed 2 for 3 minutes, then increase to speed 3 and then speed 4, until the butter is incorporated and the dough pulls away from the sides of the bowl in a smooth ball.

Add the candied fruit and the previously roasted and chopped almonds, hazelnuts and pine nuts. Knead until smooth.

RISING

Take the dough out of the mixer and shape into a ball. Place in a bowl and cover with cling film in direct contact. Leave to rise at room temperature for 2 hours.

SHAPING

Deflate the dough, then divide and weigh it out into two 400-g portions. Shape each individual piece into a ball by rolling it with the palm of your hand on the work surface. Wrap in cling film and rest for 15 minutes at room temperature.

Grease cake rings with butter and line with a strip of baking parchment. Place the rings on baking parchment. Put the dough balls into the centre of the cake rings and flatten with the back of your hand.

PROVING

Prove the brioches in an improvised proving oven at 24°C for 2 hours (see p. 24).

FOR THE ALMOND GLAZE

In a bowl, whisk the caster sugar with the egg whites. Add the ground almonds. Cover with cling film and set aside at room temperature.

FOR THE BRIOCHE DOUGH

150 g (3) eggs

117 g milk

14 g fresh yeast

330 g Italian '00' flour or plain flour

40 g caster sugar

9 g fine salt

50 g unsalted butter, softened

50 g candied fruit cubes

30 g candied lemon peel cubes

30 g candied orange peel cubes

20 g almonds

20 g hazelnuts

20 g pine nuts

FOR THE ALMOND GLAZE

65 g caster sugar

175 g egg whites

175 g ground almonds

FINISHING

Icing sugar

1 slice candied orange

1 slice candied lemon

Almonds

TIP

For a more developed brioche with an open crumb, knead your dough the night before and rest it overnight in the refrigerator.

Makes
2 medium
brioches

Preparation
time:
1 hour

Cooking time:
30–35
minutes

Resting time:
4 hours
15 minutes

BAKING AND FINISHING

Take the brioches out of the oven. Using a piping bag with a size 10 plain nozzle, cover them with the almond glaze and then dust three times with icing sugar.

Preheat the oven to 180°C (Gas Mark 4) with the oven baking tray inside. Place the brioches on the hot baking tray and bake at 165°C (Gas Mark 3) for 30–35 minutes, then turn them out on a rack. Decorate with the candied orange and lemon slices and scatter over the almonds.

COCONUT MACAROONS

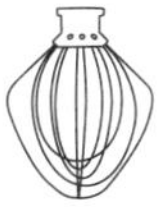

Preheat the oven to 180°C (Gas Mark 4).
Put the egg whites into the mixer fitted with the whisk and whisk on speed 8 until the whites are quite firm. Gradually add the sugar and whisk for a few seconds. The beaten egg whites should turn glossy.
Mix the grated coconut and flour in a bowl. Gently fold the egg whites into the mixture.

Using two spoons, shape the dough into balls and place them on a baking tray lined with baking parchment. Bake for about 15 minutes. Leave to cool on a rack.

4 egg whites
225 g caster sugar
225 g grated coconut
40 g plain flour

Makes about
500 g

Preparation
time:
15 minutes

Cooking time:
15 minutes

PIPED ALMOND PETIT FOUR BISCUITS

The previous day, cut the almond paste into small cubes and put into the mixer fitted with the paddle attachment. Add the honey and mix on speed 2 for 2 minutes to loosen the almond paste. Reduce to speed 1 and gradually add the egg whites. Mix until smooth.

Transfer to a piping bag fitted with a star nozzle and pipe biscuits on a baking tray lined with baking parchment. Arrange a piece of candied orange and lemon on each biscuit. Then top with half a pistachio and a pine nut.

Leave the biscuits to stand at room temperature for 12 hours to form a crust.

Preheat the oven to 200°C (Gas Mark 6). Bake for 5–7 minutes.

625 g raw almond paste (70% almonds)

15 g set multiflower honey

90 g (3) egg whites

Candied orange and lemon peel

Pistachios and pine nuts

Makes 65–70
biscuits

Preparation
time:
15 minutes

Cooking time:
5–7 minutes

Resting time:
12 hours

BRETON SHORTBREAD BISCUITS

In the mixer fitted with the whisk, mix the egg yolks with the sugar on speed 8 for 3 minutes, until very thick and pale. Add the softened butter and beat on speed 4.

Sift the flour with the baking powder and add the fleur de sel. Replace the whisk with the paddle attachment and incorporate the dry ingredients on speed 1, just enough for a soft dough to form.

Place the dough on cling film, wrap the film over the dough and shape into a sausage with a diameter of about 6 cm. Refrigerate for at least 1 hour.

Preheat the oven to 180°C (Gas Mark 4).

Cut the dough sausage into 1-cm-thick slices. Place them in the centre of the cavities in a silicone mould. Bake the biscuits at 170°C (Gas Mark 3) for 12–15 minutes, until golden.

Wait for 5 minutes before turning them out, then leave to cool on a rack.

50 g (2 large) egg yolks
100 g brown sugar
125 g semi-salted butter, softened
150 g organic plain flour
6 g baking powder
3 large pinches fleur de sel

TIP

You can also flavour your shortbread with cocoa, pistachio, etc.

Makes 6–8
biscuits

Preparation
time:
15 minutes

Cooking time:
12–15 minutes

Resting time:
1 hour

CHURROS

FOR THE CHOUX PASTRY

Melt the butter in a saucepan with the milk and 150 ml water. Remove from the heat and add the flour all at once. Mix well. Return the pan to the heat and dry out the paste until it comes away from the sides of the pan. Transfer the paste to the mixer fitted with the paddle attachment, run the mixer on speed 1 and incorporate the eggs, one at a time. The pastry should be slightly firm. Fit a piping bag with a plain nozzle and fill with the pastry.

COOKING AND FINISHING

Heat the oil for frying. As soon as it is hot, pipe the choux pastry into it by pressing on the piping bag to form churros that are 10–15 cm long. Fry for a few moments and then transfer the churros to kitchen paper. Dust each batch with raw sugar.
Serve hot with salted butter caramel, lightly heated home-made spread (see recipe on p. 34, for example) or simply melted chocolate!

FOR THE CHOUX PASTRY
120 g unsalted butter
150 ml milk
150 g plain flour
4–5 eggs

FINISHING
Vegetable oil, for frying
Raw sugar
Salted butter caramel or home-made spread (see p. 34)

TIP

Use small portions of choux pastry to check that the frying oil is hot enough.

Serves 4

Preparation
time:
20 minutes

Cooking time:
5 minutes

PALMIERS

FOR THE PUFF PASTRY
Make the puff pastry as shown on p. 17, using the quantities indicated here and making only two single turns.

On a floured work surface, make two last turns, taking care not to tear the dough. Rest the pastry for at least 30 minutes.

Roll out the pastry into a rectangle 60 cm long with a thickness of 5–6 mm. Trim the edges cleanly with a knife. Fold the two halves of the rectangle in towards the middle, leaving a space of about 1 cm between them. Fold each half twice. You can also fold each half palmier four times. Fold the two halves together like a book to leave a rectangle about 12 cm in width and 4 cm thick.

BAKING AND FINISHING
Cut the pastry into strips 1–1.5 cm wide. Arrange them on a baking tray greased with butter, spacing them far enough apart to prevent the palmiers touching each other as they bake. Spread them slightly into a V shape at the fold. Rest at room temperature for about 15 minutes.

Preheat the oven to 200°C (Gas Mark 6). Bake for 25 minutes. Turn the palmiers over halfway through so they turn golden on both sides. Transfer to a rack.

FOR THE PUFF PASTRY
185 g unsalted butter
125 g water
250 g plain flour
5 g salt
200 g caster sugar

FINISHING
75 g unsalted butter, melted

Afternoon
tea

Makes
12 large or
50 small
palmiers

Preparation
time:
1 hour

Cooking time:
25 minutes

Resting time:
2 hours
15 minutes

RASPBERRY MACARONS

FOR THE MACARON BATTER

Sift the ground almonds with the icing sugar into a large bowl.

Put the egg whites into the mixer fitted with the whisk and beat on speed 4. When they begin to form soft peaks, add the caster sugar and increase the speed to 6. Continue beating until the egg whites have the consistency of a meringue. They should form stiff peaks when you lift up the whisk.

Gently fold the sifted almond mixture into the egg whites with a rubber palette knife, then add the food colouring. The mixture should be smooth and glossy.

ASSEMBLY AND BAKING

Put the batter into a piping bag fitted with a 10- or 12-mm plain nozzle, then pipe out uniform 2.5-cm-diameter discs over a baking tray lined with baking parchment. Leave to dry out at room temperature for 30 minutes.

Preheat the oven to 150°C (Gas Mark2). Bake for 12–15 minutes. After removing the shells from the oven, leave to cool completely before lifting them off the parchment. Spread a spoonful of jam over half the shells and cover with the remaining shells. Rest the macarons in the refrigerator.

110 g ground almonds

110 g icing sugar

110 g (4 small) egg whites

120 g caster sugar

Pink food colouring powder

1 jar raspberry jam

Makes
30 macarons

Preparation
time:
15 minutes

Cooking time:
12-15 minutes

Resting time:
30 minutes

CHOCOLATE AND PEANUT COOKIES

Preheat the oven to 180°C on the fan-assisted setting (or 200°C/Gas Mark 6). Roughly chop the chocolate and peanuts with a knife.

In the mixer fitted with the pastry beater, mix the softened butter with the caster sugar and brown sugar on speed 4 for 1 minute. Add the eggs and mix for 30 seconds. Gradually add the flour, baking powder, bicarbonate of soda and fleur de sel. Mix on speed 4 for 2 minutes. Reduce to speed 1, add the chopped chocolate and peanuts, and mix for 30 seconds.

Shape the dough into balls and arrange them spaced apart on a baking tray lined with baking parchment. Flatten them slightly with the palm of your hand. Bake for 12 minutes, then check the cookies – they should be just beginning to turn golden. Leave to cool for 10 minutes before lifting them off the parchment.

200 g dark chocolate

100 g unsalted peanuts

200 g unsalted butter, very soft

100 g caster sugar

150 g brown sugar

2 eggs

370 g Italian '00' flour or plain flour

11 g baking powder

1 tsp bicarbonate of soda

1 pinch fleur de sel

TIPS

Use an ice cream scoop to make uniform dough balls. To flavour the cookies, replace 100 g of the flour with ground hazelnuts. Try using different nuts: almonds, pecans, hazelnuts, pine nuts, pistachios, etc.

Makes
25 cookies

Preparation
time:
15 minutes

Cooking time:
12 minutes

FOCACCIA
WITH OLIVES

Put the flour into the mixer fitted with the dough hook. Add the salt to one side of the bowl and crumble the yeast over the other side. Run the mixer on speed 1, then pour in 170 g of water and the olive oil. Mix on speed 1 for 2 minutes, until smooth, then increase to speed 2 and knead the dough for 7–8 minutes. Roughly chop the olives with a knife. Add them to the dough and mix on speed 1 for a further 1 minute.

Lightly grease a round cake tin with oil. Spread out the dough inside the tin by hand to distribute the filling throughout. Cover with a damp cloth and leave to rise at room temperature for 1 hour, until it doubles in size.

Preheat the oven to 200°C (Gas Mark 6). Brush the top of the focaccia with oil. Decorate with thyme sprigs and carrot slices to create a country scene. Arrange red onion rings and olive pieces to represent flowers. Sprinkle with fleur de sel. Bake for 15-20 minutes and leave to cool before serving.

300 g Italian '00' flour or plain flour

6 g salt

15 g fresh yeast (or 6 g active dried yeast)

20 g olive oil

100 g pitted black olives

10 sprigs thyme

1 yellow carrot

1 red onion

Fleur de sel

Serves 6–8

Preparation
time:
15 minutes

Cooking
time: 15–20
minutes

Resting time:
1 hour

CEREAL
BARS

Preheat the oven to 180°C (Gas Mark 4). Put all the ingredients into the mixer fitted with the pastry beater. Mix on speed 2 for 2 minutes.

Distribute the mixture among the cavities of a silicone mini loaf mould or fill a large rectangular baking dish. Compact well with the back of a spoon.

Bake for 25 minutes, until golden. Turn the bars out of the mould and leave to cool. Use a cold knife to cut out the bars if using a baking dish. Store these cereal bars in a metal box.

120 g porridge oats
40 g whole almonds
40 g cashew nuts
2 tbsp grated coconut
50 g apple sauce
60 g maple syrup
1 pinch salt

VARIATION

Use different nuts according to preference: hazelnuts, macadamia nuts, etc.

SUNDAY DESSERTS

PECAN AND
SALTED BUTTER CARAMEL
LOAF CAKE

FOR THE PECAN LOAF CAKE
Brown the butter to make a beurre noisette, then leave it to cool to room temperature in a bowl.
In the mixer fitted with the paddle attachment, beat the egg with 60 g of the brown sugar, the icing sugar, ground pecans and salt on speed 2 for 5 minutes, until thick and pale. Reduce to speed 1 and add the beurre noisette.
Sift the flour with the baking powder and add them to the mixture on speed 1 for 2 minutes, mixing until smooth. Transfer the mixture to a bowl and wash the mixer bowl.

Put the egg whites into the mixer fitted with the whisk. Beat the egg whites on speed 8, adding the remaining 12 g of brown sugar, to form stiff peaks. Gently fold the egg whites into the previous mixture with a rubber palette knife.
Preheat the oven to 160°C (Gas Mark 3). Grease a loaf tin with butter and pour in the mixture. Bake for 40 minutes.

FOR THE SALTED BUTTER CARAMEL
In a saucepan, make a dry caramel with the sugar and half vanilla pod. Deglaze the caramel with the hot cream and then add the butter. Transfer to a piping bag, leave to cool in the refrigerator and set aside for assembly.

FOR THE ICING
Melt the chocolate over a bain-marie or in the microwave. Add the oil and flaked almonds. Set aside at room temperature.

ASSEMBLY AND FINISHING
Cut the cake in half horizontally through the middle and pipe caramel over the bottom half. Cover with the top half and refrigerate for 1 hour.
Pipe a little more caramel over the cake. Chill in the freezer for 30 minutes.
Cover the cake with the almond icing heated to 30°C. Decorate the cake with pecans and gold leaf.

FOR THE PECAN LOAF CAKE
70 g unsalted butter

1 egg

60 g + 12 g brown sugar

20 g icing sugar

75 g ground roasted pecan nuts

1 pinch salt

35 g plain flour

2 g baking powder

80 g (2 large or 3 small) egg whites

FOR THE SALTED BUTTER CARAMEL
110 g caster sugar

½ vanilla pod

110 g whipping cream, freshly heated

85 g semi-salted butter

FOR THE ICING
225 g milk chocolate

25 g grapeseed oil

35 g roasted flaked almonds

FINISHING
Pecan nuts

Edible gold leaf

TIP

If your caramel is too runny, put it into the mixer fitted with the whisk and whisk to the desired consistency.

Makes 1 cake
(300 g in
weight)

Preparation
time:
45 minutes

Cooking time:
40 minutes

Resting time:
1 hour
30 minutes

PECAN BROWNIES

Preheat the oven to 180°C (Gas Mark 4). Melt the chocolate and butter over a bain-marie.
In the mixer fitted with the pastry beater, mix the eggs and sugar and on speed 4 for 1 minute. Add the melted chocolate and butter, then mix for 1 minute. Add the flour and baking powder, and mix for 2 minutes. Reduce to speed 1 and add the chopped pecans.

Line a square cake tin with baking parchment. Pour in the mixture and bake for about 30 minutes. Leave to cool before turning out.

200 g dark chocolate
200 g semi-salted butter
4 eggs
160 g caster sugar
80 g plain flour
1 tsp baking powder
100 g pecan nuts, chopped

VARIATIONS

This brownie can be made with pistachios, hazelnuts, almonds, walnuts pine nuts, etc. for a delicious variation! For a gluten-free version, substitute the wheat flour with rice flour.

Serves 6

Preparation
time:
10 minutes

Cooking time:
30 minutes

BAKED LEMON CHEESECAKE

FOR THE BASE
Preheat the oven to 160°C on the fan-assisted setting (or 180°C/Gas Mark 3).
In the mixer fitted with the pastry beater, combine the sugar, ground almonds, flour and softened butter on speed 1 until crumbly. Press the mixture into the base of a deep 20-cm-diameter springform cake tin. Bake for 10–15 minutes, until light golden. Leave to cool.

FOR THE BAKED CHEESECAKE
Reduce the oven temperature to 90°C (Gas Mark ¼). Clean the mixer bowl and add the cream cheese. Using the paster beater, run the mixer on speed 1 and work the cheese until soft. Then add one ingredient at a time in the following order: sugar, lightly beaten eggs, sifted flour, crème fraîche, grated lemon zest and juice. The mixture should be only lightly beaten, so allow just 10–20 seconds between each addition. When smooth, pour the mixture over the base. Bake for 1 hour.

When baked, the cheesecake should still be wobbly in the centre. Turn off the oven, hold the door ajar with the handle of a wooden spoon and leave the cheesecake for 30 minutes to set. Take the cheesecake out of the oven and wait for it to cool completely, then refrigerate for at least 10 hours.

FOR THE BASE
55 g caster sugar
55 g ground almonds
55 g plain flour
35 g unsalted butter, very soft

FOR THE CHEESECAKE MIXTURE
600 g cream cheese, at room temperature
150 g caster sugar
2 eggs
25 g plain flour
150 g crème fraîche
2 organic lemons

TIP
Serve this cheesecake accompanied by a mixed berry fruit salad.

Serves 8

Preparation
time:
30 minutes

Cooking time:
1 hour
15 minutes

Resting time:
10 hours
30 minutes

SUGAR TARTS

FOR THE DOUGH
Make the brioche dough as described on p. 14.

RISING
Take the dough out of the mixer and shape it into a ball. Place it in a large bowl and cover with cling film in direct contact. Leave to rise at room temperature for 1 hour.
Deflate the dough, then shape it into a ball. Wrap the dough in cling film. Refrigerate for 2 hours.

SHAPING
Deflate the dough, then divide and weigh it out into 13 portions of 60 g each. Roll the pieces into balls with the palm of your hand on the work surface, cover them with cling film and rest for 5 minutes at room temperature. Roll the dough balls again and refrigerate for 20 minutes.
With a rolling pin, roll each dough ball into a 12-cm-diameter disc. Lay the discs on baking parchment. Brush the tops of the tarts with the beaten egg.

PROVING
Prove the tarts in an improvised proving oven at 24°C for 1 hour (see p. 24).

ASSEMBLY AND BAKING
Take the tarts out of the oven and rest at room temperature for 10 minutes. Preheat the oven to 180°C (Gas Mark 4) with the oven baking tray inside.
Glaze the tarts again with the beaten egg. Place 5 small cubes of butter on each tart and sprinkle generously with the brown or light brown beet sugar. Place the tarts on the hot baking tray and bake at 180°C (Gas Mark 4) for 10–12 minutes. Transfer to a rack.

FOR THE BRIOCHE DOUGH
200 g (4) eggs
15 g fresh yeast
330 g Italian '00' flour or plain flour
60 g caster sugar
7 g fine salt
170 g unsalted butter
1 beaten egg, for glazing

FOR THE TOPPING
260 g semi-salted butter
130 g brown sugar or light brown beet sugar

VARIATION

You can replace the butter with crème fraîche and lemon zest.

Makes
13 individual
tarts

Preparation
time:
45 minutes

Cooking time:
12 minutes

Resting time:
4 hours
35 minutes

BRIOCHE TATIN

FOR THE DOUGH

Make the brioche dough as described on p. 14 using the quantities given here.

RISING

Take the dough out of the mixer and shape it into a ball. Place it in a bowl and cover with cling film in direct contact. Leave to rise at room temperature for 1 hour. Deflate the dough, then shape it into a ball. Wrap the dough in cling film. Refrigerate for 2 hours.

APPLES

Peel, core and halve the apples.

FOR THE CARAMEL

In a saucepan, make a dry caramel as follows: put a third of the sugar into a saucepan and melt over a low heat. When the first batch of sugar is melted, add the next, then repeat this operation with the remaining sugar. Cook the caramel to a dark amber colour.
Remove from the heat and add the butter, cut into small cubes. Whisk the butter into the caramel until smooth. Pour the caramel into a deep round cake tin.

FOR THE FILLING

Preheat the oven to 175°C (Gas Mark 3¾). Arrange the apple halves on their sides in the caramel, packing them tightly in a rosette pattern. Scatter over brown sugar and add small cubes of butter.
Bake for 35–40 minutes. When the apples are cooked and turn deep golden, take them out of the oven and increase the oven to heat to 180°C (Gas Mark 4). Leave the apples to cool to room temperature.

SHAPING THE BRIOCHE

Deflate the dough, then roll it into a ball with the palm of your hand on the work surface. Refrigerate for 5 minutes. With a rolling pin, roll out the dough into a disc the same size as the cake tin. Lay the dough disc over the still-warm caramelised apples.

PROVING

Prove the brioche at room temperature for 10 minutes.

FOR THE BRIOCHE DOUGH
100 g (2) eggs
7 g fresh yeast
165 g Italian '00' flour or plain flour
30 g caster sugar
3 g fine salt
85 g unsalted butter

FOR THE FILLING
6 Golden Delicious apples
Brown sugar
Unsalted butter

FOR THE CARAMEL
75 g caster sugar
75 g semi-salted butter

FINISHING
Caramelised hazelnuts

TIP
When the apples come out of the oven, you can lightly brush them with a neutral glaze to make them nice and glossy.

Makes
1 medium
brioche

Preparation
time:
1 hour

Cooking time:
1 hour

Resting time:
3 hours
15 minutes

BAKING AND FINISHING
Bake the brioche at 180°C for 10–15 minutes, then remove from the oven and place on a rack. When cold, turn the brioche out of the mould onto a plate. Coat the edge of the brioche with caramelised hazelnuts.

BRIOCHE TART
WITH MIXED BERRIES AND CRUMBLE TOPPING

FOR THE CRUMBLE TOPPING
In the mixer fitted with the pastry beater, combine the butter, sugar and flour on speed 2 and mix until the dough has a uniform, crumbly consistency. Refrigerate.

FOR THE DOUGH
Make the brioche dough as described on p. 14.

RISING
Take the dough out of the mixer and shape it into a ball. Place it in a bowl and cover with cling film in direct contact. Leave to rise at room temperature for 1 hour. Deflate the dough, then shape it into a ball. Wrap the dough in cling film. Refrigerate for 2 hours.

SHAPING
Deflate the dough, then divide and weigh it out into three portions of 260 g each. With a rolling pin, roll out each piece to a thickness of about 5 mm. Use a 20-cm square baking frame to cut out the tart bases.
Grease the baking frames with butter. Lay each frame on baking parchment, then fill with the brioche dough squares. Brush the top of the brioches with beaten egg.

PROVING
Prove the brioches in an improvised proving oven at 24°C for 1 hour (see p. 24).

FOR THE TOPPING
Take the brioches out of the oven. Glaze the top again with the beaten egg. Quarter the strawberries and make an attractive arrangement with them and all the other berries on top of the brioches. Roughly crumble the crumble mixture over the berries.

BAKING AND FINISHING
Preheat the oven to 190°C (Gas Mark 5) with the oven baking tray inside. Place the brioche tarts on the hot baking tray and bake at 180°C (Gas Mark 4) for 10–12 minutes.
Transfer to a rack. When cold, scatter icing sugar over the brioche tarts and decorate with mixed berries.

FOR THE CRUMBLE
115 g unsalted butter
135 g brown sugar
135 g plain flour

FOR THE BRIOCHE DOUGH
200 g (4) eggs
15 g fresh yeast
330 g Italian '00' flour or plain flour
60 g caster sugar
7 g fine salt
170 g unsalted butter
1 egg, for glazing

FOR THE TOPPING
250 g strawberries
125 g raspberries
125 g blueberries
125 g redcurrants
Wild strawberries and blackberries

FINISHING
Icing sugar
Mixed berries

VARIATION

You can use spelt flour to make the crumble topping; it will be delicious!

Makes
3 medium
brioche tarts

Preparation
time:
50 minutes

Cooking time:
10-12 minutes

Resting time:
4 hours

CHOCOLATE AND MANDARIN BRIOCHE TART

FOR THE MANDARIN PASTRY CREAM
325 g mandarin purée
40 g caster sugar
60 g (3) egg yolks
25 g cornflour

FOR THE CHOCOLATE BUTTER
170 g unsalted butter
100 g dark chocolate

FOR THE BRIOCHE DOUGH
200 g (4) eggs
15 g fresh yeast
330 g Italian '00' flour or plain flour
60 g caster sugar
7 g fine salt
1 beaten egg, for glazing

FINISHING
Brown sugar
1 orange slice
Icing sugar
Mint leaves
Zest of 1 lime

Makes
2 medium
tarts

Preparation
time:
50 minutes

Cooking time:
22-25 minutes

Resting time:
5 hours

FOR THE MANDARIN PASTRY CREAM

Combine the mandarin purée and half the sugar in a saucepan over the heat.

In a bowl, blanch the egg yolks by whisking them with the remaining caster sugar until soft and pale. Add the cornflour and mix again. When the mandarin purée comes to the boil, mix a small amount into the blanched egg yolks.

Return the mixture to the pan and cook, stirring constantly, over a low heat for 4 minutes.

Transfer the pastry cream to a dish, cover with cling film in direct contact and chill in the freezer for 15–20 minutes.

When cold, set aside in the refrigerator.

FOR THE CHOCOLATE BUTTER

Cut the butter into small cubes and soften lightly in the microwave. Whisk the butter to a creamy consistency. Melt the chocolate over a bain-marie. Check the temperature of the chocolate: the ideal temperature for this mixture is 35°C. Once the chocolate is at the right temperature, mix it with the butter. Refrigerate.

When cold, cut the chocolate butter into small cubes and set aside at room temperature.

FOR THE DOUGH

Make the brioche dough as described on p. 14 using the chocolate butter.

RISING

Take the dough out of the mixer and shape it into a ball. Place it in a bowl and cover with cling film in direct contact. Leave to rise at room temperature for 2 hours. Deflate the dough, then shape it into a ball and wrap in cling film. Refrigerate for 2 hours.

TIP

If you have one, you can use a size 15 plain nozzle to pipe the pastry cream.

FOR THE TARTS

With a rolling pin, roll out the dough to a thickness of 3 mm. Chill the dough in the freezer for 15 minutes.
Take the dough out of the freezer and, while still cold, cut out four 18-cm-diameter discs. Lay two discs on baking parchment and glaze with the beaten egg.
Use a 16-cm-diameter biscuit cutter to cut out the centre of the two remaining discs. Lay the two dough rings over the two complete discs. Brush the rims with the beaten egg.
Use a piping bag to fill the inside of the tarts with the mandarin pastry cream. Scatter brown sugar over the rims of the tarts.

PROVING

Prove the tarts at room temperature for about 15 minutes.

BAKING AND FINISHING

Preheat the oven to 200°C (Gas Mark 6) with the oven baking tray inside. Place the tarts on the hot baking tray and bake at 180°C (Gas Mark 4) for 15–18 minutes. Transfer the tarts to a rack and leave to cool. Place a very thin orange slice in the centre of each cold brioche tart and dust around the edges with icing sugar. To finish, decorate with mint leaves and grated lime zest.

STRAWBERRY TART
WITH CHANTILLY CREAM

or

FOR THE SWEET SHORTCRUST PASTRY
Make the pastry as described on p. 15 using the ingredients and quantities given here. Form the dough into a ball, wrap it in cling film and refrigerate for 1 hour. Roll out the pastry with a rolling pin, prick with a fork and line a 20-cm-diameter tart ring greased with butter. Refrigerate.

FOR THE ALMOND AND PISTACHIO CREAM
In the mixer fitted with the paddle attachment, beat the butter on speed 4 until soft and creamy. Add the sugar and mix for 1 minute on speed 4. Add the beaten egg, then incorporate the ground almonds and pistachio paste and increase to speed 4 for 2 minutes. Fill the tart case with the almond and pistachio cream. Smooth with an angled palette knife.

FOR THE TOPPING
Preheat the oven to 180°C (Gas Mark 4).
Hull the strawberries, then cut 4 or 5 into quarters. Keep 16–18 whole and cut the remainder in half. Arrange about 15 strawberry quarters over the almond and pistachio cream. Add about 15 pistachios. Bake in the oven for 30–40 minutes. Leave to cool completely.
Use an angled palette knife to cover with a layer of raspberry jam.

FOR THE MASCARPONE CHANTILLY CREAM
In the mixer fitted with the whisk, whisk the chilled cream with the mascarpone and scraped vanilla seeds on speed 8. When soft peaks form, add the icing sugar. Whisk again until the cream is fully whipped.
Transfer to a piping bag fitted with a star nozzle. Pipe a line of cream about 5 mm wide in a spiral over the tart.

FOR THE SWEET SHORTCRUST PASTRY
100 g semi-salted butter
70 g icing sugar
1 g salt
35 g (1 small) egg
175 g plain flour
28 g ground almonds

FOR THE ALMOND AND PISTACHIO CREAM
50 g unsalted butter
50 g caster sugar
50 g (1) egg
50 g ground almonds
10 g pistachio paste

FOR THE TOPPING
250 g strawberries
15–20 pistachios
75 g raspberry jam

FOR THE MASCARPONE CHANTILLY CREAM
310 g whipping cream
190 g mascarpone cheese
2 vanilla pods, split and scraped
40 g icing sugar

FINISHING
50 g neutral glaze
10 g ground pistachios
Edible gold leaf
Toasted pistachios
Wild strawberries
Icing sugar
Sugar paste flowers

TIP
If you prefer, make an all-pistachio cream by using ground pistachios instead of ground almonds.

Makes 1 tart
(20 cm in
diameter)

Preparation
time:
1 hour
20 minutes

Cooking time:
30–40 minutes

Resting time:
1 hour

FINISHING

Arrange whole strawberries in a circle around the edge of the tart. Make a second circle with the strawberry halves, then a third, until the cream is covered. Brush the edge of the tart and the strawberries with the neutral glaze.

Cover the sides of the tart completely with the ground pistachios. Use a star nozzle to pipe a swirl of cream in the middle of the tart, giving it volume.

Add the garnishes: gold leaf, toasted pistachios, wild strawberries dusted with icing sugar through a small sieve, sugar paste flowers, etc.

CHOCOLATE TART

or

FOR THE SWEET COCOA SHORTCRUST PASTRY
Make the pastry as described on p. 15 using the ingredients and quantities given here.
Roll the dough out to a thickness of 3 mm. Prick the pastry with a fork and line a 20-cm-diameter tart ring greased with butter. Chill the tart case for 10 minutes in the freezer or 1 hour in the refrigerator.
Preheat the oven to 180°C (Gas Mark 4). Blind bake the pastry case for 30 minutes. If necessary, scrape the edges of the tart case with a paring knife to make it smoother. Place the baked tart case on a baking tray.

FOR THE CHOCOLATE GANACHE
In a saucepan, combine the cream with the glucose and bring to the boil. Pour the mixture over the chocolate, either chopped or in drops (chips). Mix with a rubber palette knife. Cut the butter into cubes and incorporate, then mix until glossy and with a ribbon consistency. Pour the ganache into the tart case. Leave to cool and set in the refrigerator for 30 minutes.

FOR THE CHOCOLATE MIRROR GLAZE
Soften the gelatine leaves in a bowl of very cold water. In a saucepan, combine 280 g of water with the sugar and bring to the boil to make a syrup.

Add the cocoa powder, mix and bring to a boil, stirring with a rubber palette knife. Whisk in the cream. Cook at a boil over a medium heat, whisking constantly, for 7 minutes. Remove from the heat and add the softened and drained gelatine. Strain through a chinois sieve into a small bowl. Use the glaze at 28–29°C.

Place the tart on a rack positioned inside a large dish. Pour the mirror glaze over the tart. Use a palette knife to spread and smooth the glaze evenly. Prick any air bubbles with a knife tip. Leave to set for about 5 minutes.

FINISHING
Decorate with gold leaf and sugar paste flowers.

FOR THE SWEET COCOA SHORTCRUST PASTRY
100 g semi-salted butter

70 g icing sugar

1 g salt

40 g eggs

150 g plain flour

28 g ground almonds

25 g cocoa powder

FOR THE CHOCOLATE GANACHE
190 g whipping cream

20 g glucose syrup

150 g dark couverture chocolate (70%)

25 g semi-salted butter

FOR THE CHOCOLATE MIRROR GLAZE
7 gelatine leaves (14 g)

360 g caster sugar

120 g cocoa powder

210 g whipping cream

FINISHING
Edible gold leaf
Sugar paste flowers

TIP
If You do not have glucose syrup at home, you can use honey.

Makes 1 tart (20 cm in diameter)

Preparation time: 1 hour

Cooking time: 40 minutes

Resting time: 2 hours 35 minutes

BERRY TIRAMISU

FOR THE BERRY COULIS
To make the mixed berry coulis, put the berries into the mixer fitted with the pastry beater and purée on speed 4. Transfer to a saucepan, add the sugar and bring to the boil. Leave to cool.

FOR THE TIRAMISU MIXTURE
Separate the egg whites from the yolks. In the mixer fitted with the whisk, whisk the egg yolks with 25 g of the sugar on speed 4 for 3 minutes. Add the mascarpone and continue to whisk for 2 minutes. Transfer to a large bowl and set aside.

Put the egg whites into the clean mixer bowl and whisk on speed 1, gradually increasing it to speed 8. When they begin to hold soft peaks, incorporate the remaining 25 g sugar, a little at a time. When stiff peaks form, fold the beaten egg whites into the mascarpone mix with a rubber palette knife.

ASSEMBLY AND FINISHING
Quickly dip the sponge fingers into the berry coulis. In a large baking dish, make a bed of whole berries, then cover with the tiramisu mixture and add a layer of sponge fingers. Cover with another layer of tiramisu mixture, followed by sponge fingers, coulis and fresh fruit, finishing with a final layer of tiramisu mixture. Serve chilled.

or

FOR THE BERRY COULIS
300 g mixed berries
20 g caster sugar

FOR THE TIRAMISU MIXTURE
2 eggs
50 g caster sugar
250 g mascarpone cheese

FINISHING
150 g mixed berries
About 20 sponge fingers

Serves 6

Preparation
time:
20 minutes

Cooking time:
5 minutes

PEACH AND REDCURRANT BRIOCHE TART

FOR THE DOUGH

Make the brioche dough as described on p. 14 using the quantities given here.

RISING

Take the dough out of the mixer and shape it into a ball. Place it in a large bowl and cover with cling film in direct contact. Leave to rise at room temperature for 1 hour.
Deflate the dough, then shape it into a ball. Wrap the dough in cling film. Refrigerate for 2 hours.

FOR THE ALMOND CREAM

In the mixer fitted with the paddle attachment, beat the almond paste, sugar, egg, egg yolk and bitter almond extract on speed 2 until very smooth. Add the flour and mix on speed 2 for 2 minutes. Transfer to a large bowl and cover with cling film in direct contact. Refrigerate.

FOR THE TARTS

Deflate the dough, then divide and weigh it out into two portions of 195 g each. With a rolling pin, roll out each piece into a 20-cm square. Grease tart rings with butter and place them on baking parchment. Fit each dough square into a tart ring.
Use a piping bag to cover with almond cream.
Wash and cut the peaches into wedges. Arrange the peach wedges in a rosette pattern and scatter over the currants. Scatter lightly with brown sugar.

BAKING AND FINISHING

Preheat the oven to 170°C (Gas Mark 3½) with the oven baking tray inside. Place the tarts on the hot baking tray and bake at 160°C (Gas Mark 3) for 25–30 minutes. Transfer the tarts to a rack and leave to cool.
When cold, brush the peaches with neutral glaze and decorate with redcurrants and verbena leaves. Dust the edges of the tarts with icing sugar.

FOR THE BRIOCHE DOUGH

100 g (2) eggs
7 g fresh yeast
165 g Italian '00' flour or plain flour
30 g caster sugar
3 g fine salt
85 g unsalted butter

FOR THE ALMOND CREAM

112 g almond paste (50% almonds)
35 g caster sugar
50 g (1) egg
20 g (1) egg yolk
2 g bitter almond extract
25 g plain flour

FOR THE TOPPING AND FINISHING

Peaches
Redcurrants
Brown sugar
Neutral glaze
Verbena leaves
Icing sugar

TIPS

You can use mint leaves instead of verbena.
If you have one, use a size 15 plain nozzle to cover the tarts with almond cream.

Makes
2 medium
tarts

Preparation
time:
50 minutes

Cooking time:
25–30
minutes

Resting time:
3 hours

TARTE TROPÉZIENNE

FOR THE BRIOCHE DOUGH
200 g (4) eggs
15 g fresh yeast
330 g Italian '00' flour or plain flour
60 g caster sugar
7 g fine salt
170 g unsalted butter
1 beaten egg, for glazing

FOR THE NOUGATINE
80 g chestnut honey
80 g caster sugar
Zest of 1 orange
80 g unsalted butter
80 g flaked almonds

FOR THE DIPLOMAT CREAM
2 gelatine leaves (4 g)
350 g milk
1 vanilla pod
50 g caster sugar
60 g (3) egg yolks
35 g cornflour
380 g whipping cream (30% fat)

FINISHING
Icing sugar

Makes
2 medium
brioches

Preparation
time:
1 hour
10 minutes

Cooking time:
25 minutes

Resting time:
5 hours
25 minutes

TARTE
TROPÉZIENNE

FOR THE DOUGH
Make the brioche dough as described on p. 14.

RISING
Take the dough out of the mixer and shape it into a ball. Place it in a large bowl and cover with cling film in direct contact. Leave to rise at room temperature for 1 hour.
Deflate the dough, then shape it into a ball. Wrap the dough in cling film. Refrigerate for 2 hours.

FOR THE NOUGATINE
In a saucepan, heat the honey with the sugar. Add the grated orange zest and the butter. Bring to the boil for 10 seconds, then add the flaked almonds. Leave to cool at room temperature.

FOR THE TARTS
Deflate the dough, then divide and weigh it out into two portions of 350 g each. Shape the individual pieces into balls by rolling them with the palm of your hand on the work surface. Wrap them in cling film and rest for 5 minutes at room temperature.
Roll the dough balls again and refrigerate for 10 minutes. With a rolling pin, roll each dough ball into a disc 20 cm in diameter. Grease tart rings with butter and line with a strip of baking parchment, then place them on baking parchment.
Fit the dough discs into the two tart rings.
Brush the top of the dough with the beaten egg, taking care not to let any drip down the sides.

PROVING
Prove the brioches in an improvised proving oven at 24°C for 2 hours (see p. 24).

TIPS

For a more traditional version, replace the nougatine with a crumble topping or pearl sugar. If you have one, you can use a size 15 plain nozzle to fill the brioches with diplomat cream.

ASSEMBLY AND BAKING

Take the brioches out of the oven and rest at room temperature for 10 minutes. Preheat the oven to 180°C (Gas Mark 4) with the oven baking tray inside.

Spoon the nougatine over the top of the brioches. Place on the hot baking tray and bake at 175°C (Gas Mark 3¾) for 15–18 minutes. Transfer to a rack and leave to cool.

FOR THE DIPLOMAT CREAM

Soften the gelatine leaves in a bowl of cold water. Combine the milk, scraped vanilla seeds and half the sugar in a saucepan over the heat.

In a large bowl, blanch the egg yolks by whisking them with the remaining sugar until thick and pale. Add the cornflour and incorporate.

When the milk comes to the boil, mix a small amount into the blanched egg yolks. Return the mixture to the pan and cook, stirring continuously, over a low heat for 4 minutes.

Remove from heat and mix in the softened and drained gelatine. Transfer the pastry cream to a dish, cover with cling film in direct contact and chill in the freezer for 15–20 minutes.

When cold, set aside in the refrigerator. In the mixer fitted with the whisk, whisk the cream. Whisk the pastry cream in the bowl to smooth. Gently fold the whipped cream into the pastry cream with a rubber palette knife.

FINISHING

Use a serrated knife to cut the brioches in half through the middle. Use a piping bag to pipe large balls of diplomat cream over the bottom halves. Replace their caps. Decorate with a dusting of icing sugar.

FLOATING ISLANDS

FOR THE CUSTARD (CRÈME ANGLAISE)
Make the custard as indicated on p. 18, mixing the praline with the milk.

FOR THE MERINGUE
Preheat the oven to 180°C (Gas Mark 4). In the mixer fitted with the whisk, beat the egg whites on speed 1, gradually increasing it to speed 8. When they begin to hold soft peaks, incorporate the sugar, a little at a time. When firm peaks form, spread out the beaten egg whites in a round cake tin and bake for 3 minutes. Leave to cool.

ASSEMBLY
Pour the custard into soup plates or bowls, then add 1–2 tablespoons of the meringue. Sprinkle with praline and serve chilled.

**FOR THE CUSTARD
(CRÈME ANGLAISE)**
6 egg yolks
100 g sugar
500 ml semi-skimmed milk
2 tsp praline

FOR THE MERINGUE
6 egg whites
80 g caster sugar

ASSEMBLY
2 tbsp praline

TIP
You can sprinkle the meringue with cocoa powder, caramel, flaked almonds, etc.

SERVES 4-6

Preparation
time:
10 minutes

Cooking time:
8 minutes

AMANDINE TART WITH RASPBERRIES

FOR THE SHORTCRUST PASTRY

In the mixer fitted with the paddle attachment, combine the butter, flour, salt, sugar and scraped vanilla seeds on speed 2 until a crumbly consistency. Add the egg and milk. Mix quickly until a ball forms. Use a rubber palette knife to scrape the pastry together and wrap in cling film. Rest for 1 hour in the refrigerator or 10 minutes in the freezer.

Roll out the pastry with a rolling pin. Prick it all over with a fork. Line an 18-cm-diameter tart ring greased with butter with the pastry and place on a baking tray.

FOR THE ALMOND CREAM

Preheat the oven to 170°C (Gas Mark 3½).
In the mixer fitted with the paddle attachment, beat the butter on speed 4 until creamy. Add the sugar and scraped vanilla seeds, then mix on speed 4 for 1 minute. Add the beaten egg, then incorporate the ground almonds, flour and rum on speed 4 for 2 minutes.
Crumble the frozen raspberries and add to the almond cream. Mix with a rubber palette knife. Fill the tart case with the almond cream. Smooth with an angled palette knife. Scatter over the flaked almonds. Bake for 30–35 minutes, then transfer to a rack and leave to cool.

FINISHING

Spread a layer of raspberry jam over the tart. Smooth with an angled palette knife. Brush the rim and sides of the tart with neutral glaze. Cover with coconut flakes. Arrange fresh raspberries in a circle around the edge of the tart. Dust them with icing sugar through a small sieve. Partially dip a few raspberries in icing sugar and decorate the middle of the tart with them together with a few mint leaves.

FOR THE SHORTCRUST PASTRY

150 g unsalted butter

250 g plain flour

5 g salt

10 g icing sugar

½ vanilla pod, split and scraped

50 g (1) egg

25 g milk

FOR THE ALMOND CREAM

65 g unsalted butter

35 g caster sugar

½ vanilla pod, split and scraped

50 g (1) egg

65 g ground almonds

5 g plain flour

5 g rum

125 g frozen raspberries

10 g flaked almonds

FINISHING

100 g raspberry jam

30 g neutral glaze

25 g coconut flakes (chips)

125 g fresh raspberries

Icing sugar

Mint leaves

TIP

You can vary the fruits, but choose ones that don't contain too much water, such as pears, apples, blueberries and cherries.

Makes 1 tart
(18 cm in
diameter)

Preparation
time:
45 minutes

Cooking time:
30–35
minutes

Resting time:
1 hour

SPECIAL OCCASIONS

BLACK FOREST ENTREMETS

FOR THE CHOCOLATE SACHER SPONGE CAKE
100 g almond paste (50% almonds)
125 g caster sugar
50 g (1) egg
65 g (3) egg yolks
90 g egg whites (3 egg whites)
30 g plain flour
30 g cocoa powder
30 g unsalted butter, melted

FOR THE CHOCOLATE GANACHE
90 g whipping cream
90 g dark couverture chocolate
20 g unsalted butter

FOR THE VANILLA CRÈME MADAME
210 g milk
1 vanilla pod, split and scraped
30 g caster sugar
22 g (1) egg yolk
15 g custard powder
18 g cocoa butter
300 g whipping cream

FOR THE SOAKING SYRUP
50 g caster sugar
40 g amarena cherry syrup

ASSEMBLY AND FINISHING
175 g amarena cherries or kirsch-soaked morello cherries
20 g unsweetened cocoa powder
150 g chocolate decorations

FOR THE MASCARPONE CHANTILLY CREAM
160 g whipping cream
95 g Mascarpone cheese
1 vanilla pod, split and scraped
20 g icing sugar

Serves 8
(makes
1 entremets/
20 in cm
diameter)

Preparation
time:
1 hour
30 minutes

Cooking time:
25 minutes

Resting time:
15 minutes

FOR THE CHOCOLATE SACHER SPONGE CAKE

Preheat the oven to 175°C (Gas Mark 3¾).
Cut the almond paste into pieces. Lightly soften by heating in the microwave. In the mixer fitted with the paddle attachment, combine the almond paste with 50 g of the caster sugar on speed 2 until smooth. Add the whole egg and the beaten yolks.
Replace the paddle attachment with the whisk. Beat on speed 4 until glossy and with a ribbon consistency. Transfer to a large bowl and wash the mixer bowl.
In the mixer fitted with the whisk, beat the egg whites on speed 8 to stiff peaks while adding the remaining 75 g of sugar, a little at a time.
Fold the beaten egg whites into the almond paste mixture with a rubber palette knife. Sift the flour with the cocoa powder and gently fold them into the mixture. Incorporate the melted butter.
Grease a 20-cm-diameter cake ring with butter and place on a baking tray lined with baking parchment. Fill with the mixture. Bake for 25 minutes, then transfer to a rack.

FOR THE CHOCOLATE GANACHE

Bring the cream to the boil. Pour it over the chopped chocolate. Mix the ganache until smooth without incorporating any air. Incorporate the butter, cut into pieces. Fill a piping bag fitted with a plain nozzle and refrigerate.

FOR THE VANILLA CRÈME MADAME

Combine the milk, scraped vanilla seeds and half the sugar in a saucepan over the heat. In a large bowl, blanch the egg yolk by whisking them with the remaining sugar until thick and pale. Add the custard powder and mix again.
When the milk comes to the boil, mix a small amount into the blanched egg yolk. Then return the mixture to the pan. Cook, stirring constantly, over a low heat for 4 minutes, until the cream thickens. Incorporate the cocoa butter. Transfer the cream to a large dish, cover with cling film in direct contact and cool in the freezer. Whip the cream in the mixer on speed 8 to soft peaks. When the temperature of the pastry cream drops to 30°C, fold in the whipped cream. Cover with cling film in direct contact and set aside in the refrigerator while you make the syrup.

TIP

You can make a more traditional version by using Chantilly mascarpone cream instead of crème madame.

FOR THE SOAKING SYRUP

Combine 110 g of water and the sugar in a saucepan and bring to the boil. Leave to cool, then add the amarena syrup. Set aside at room temperature.

ASSEMBLY

Use a serrated knife to cut twice horizontally through the middle of the Sacher sponge to make three discs. Brush the discs with the syrup to soak.

Line the same cake ring used to bake the sponge with a strip of acetate and use a palette knife to cover the strip with a 1-cm-thick layer of crème madame. Place the first sponge disc in the centre of the ring.

Pipe a spiral of ganache over the disc. Place the second disc on top and press lightly. Cover with a little crème madame and smooth with the palette knife. Set aside eight cherries for decorating the top, then arrange the remaining cherries evenly distributed over the cream.

Place the third disc on top and press lightly. Cover with crème madame to the top of the cake ring and smooth again. Chill in the freezer for 15 minutes.

FOR THE MASCARPONE CHANTILLY CREAM

Prepare the cream as indicated on p. 186 with the quantities indicated here (see p. 172).

Fit one piping bag with a plain nozzle and another with a star nozzle, then fill both bags with the cream. Refrigerate.

FINISHING

Lift the ring off the cake and use an angled palette knife to transfer the cake to a cake board. Pipe an attractive arrangement of Chantilly cream mounds over the top of the entremets, alternating between plain mounds and swirls. Using a small sieve, dust over with the cocoa powder and icing sugar. Decorate with the remaining cherries and chocolate decorations.

SAINT-HONORÉ
WITH RASPBERRIES

FOR THE PUFF PASTRY
200 g puff pastry (see p. 17)

FOR THE CHOUX PASTRY
75 g plain flour
125 g milk or water
5 g caster sugar
2 g salt
50 g unsalted butter
125 g (3 small) eggs
1 beaten egg, for glazing

FOR THE PASTRY CREAM
2 gelatine leaves (4 g)
250 g milk
2 vanilla pods, split and scraped
40 g caster sugar
120 g (6) egg yolks
20 g custard powder

FOR THE ITALIAN MERINGUE
110 g caster sugar
75 g (2 large or 3 small) egg whites

FOR THE VANILLA CHIBOUST CREAM
220 g pastry cream (see above)
225 g Italian meringue (see above)

FOR THE CARAMEL
200 g caster sugar
40 g glucose syrup

FOR THE TONKA BEAN CHANTILLY CREAM
250 g whipping cream
150 g mascarpone cheese
30 g icing sugar
1 tonka bean

FINISHING
125 g red and yellow raspberries
Icing sugar
Edible gold leaf

Serves 6
(18 cm in
diameter)

Preparation
time:
1 hour
30 minutes

Cooking time:
1 hour
15 minutes

Resting time:
2 hours
15 minutes

PUFF PASTRY
Make the puff pastry as described on p. 17. Roll out the pastry to a thickness of 2 mm. Prick the pastry all over and cut out an 18-cm-diameter disc. Refrigerate.

FOR THE CHOUX PASTRY
Preheat the oven to 170°C (Gas Mark 3½).
Make the choux pastry as described on p. 14 using the ingredients and quantities given here (see p. 176).
Transfer to a piping bag fitted with a size 10 plain nozzle. Pipe a ring of choux pastry over the edge of the puff pastry disc. Bake for 35 minutes.
On a baking sheet covered with baking parchment, pipe 2-cm-diameter choux buns in staggered rows. Glaze the choux buns by brushing them with beaten egg. Bake for 25–30 minutes. Leave to cool on a rack.

FOR THE PASTRY CREAM
Make the pastry cream as described on p. 19 using the ingredients and quantities given here (see p. 176).

ITALIAN MERINGUE
Make the Italian meringue as shown on p. 18 using the ingredients and quantities given here (see p. 176).

FOR THE VANILLA CHIBOUST CREAM
Weigh out 220 g of the pastry cream. Add the warm Italian meringue to the still-hot pastry cream after adding the gelatine. Transfer the Chiboust cream to a piping bag fitted with a plain nozzle.
Use a size 6 stainless steel star nozzle to make a hole in the base of each choux bun. Fill the choux buns with Chiboust cream.

FOR THE CARAMEL
In a saucepan, combine the sugar, 70 g of water and the glucose, and heat to 155°C to make a caramel. Glaze each choux bun by dipping the top part into the caramel. Place the Saint-Honoré inside a tart ring. Arrange the choux buns in a circle on the choux pastry ring, gluing them with caramel. Pipe Chiboust cream over the puff pastry inside the choux pastry ring.

T I P

If you do not have glucose syrup at home, you can substitute it with the same weight in granulated sugar.

FOR THE TONKA BEAN CHANTILLY CREAM
In the mixer bowl, add the cream, mascarpone and sugar, then grate in the tonka bean. Chill the bowl in the refrigerator for about 10 minutes.
Return the bowl to the mixer fitted with the whisk and whisk the cream on speed 10. Transfer the Chantilly cream to a piping bag fitted with a Saint-Honoré nozzle.

ASSEMBLY AND FINISHING
Arrange a few raspberries on the Chiboust cream. Decorate with the Chantilly cream: first, pipe a spiral layer. Then pipe the typical line decorations over the top, forming a mound. Top with a choux bun, then decorate with raspberries dusted in icing sugar and add gold leaf.

PARIS-BREST

FOR THE PASTRY CREAM
250 g milk
1 vanilla pod
25 g caster sugar
50 g (1) egg
25 g custard powder

FOR THE CHOUX PASTRY
150 g plain flour
125 g water
125 g milk
100 g unsalted butter
4 g caster sugar
4 g salt
250 g (5) eggs
1 beaten egg, for glazing
Flaked almonds

FOR THE FEULLETINE PRALINE
50 g milk chocolate
160 g praline
15 g unsalted butter
100 g pailleté feuilletine (crêpe dentelle flakes)

FOR THE PARIS-BREST CREAM
150 g unsalted butter, softened
300 g pastry cream (see opposite)
75 g praline

FINISHING
Gold sugar almonds
Icing sugar

Serves 6
(18 cm in
diameter)

Preparation
time:
1 hour
15 minutes

Cooking time:
1 hour
45 minutes

Resting time:
1 hour–1 hour
20 minutes

FOR THE PASTRY CREAM

Combine the milk, scraped vanilla seeds and half the sugar in a saucepan over the heat. In a large bowl, blanch the egg by whisking it with the remaining sugar until thick and pale. Mix in the custard powder.

When the milk comes to the boil, mix a small amount into the blanched egg, then return the mixture to the pan. Cook over a low heat, stirring constantly, for 4 minutes, until the cream thickens. Transfer to a large dish and cover with cling film in direct contact. Set aside for about 1 hour in the refrigerator or 20 minutes in the freezer.

FOR THE CHOUX PASTRY

Preheat the oven to 165°C (Gas Mark 3¾). Make the choux pastry as described on p. 14 using the ingredients and quantities given here (see p. 180).

Transfer to a piping bag fitted with a plain nozzle. On a baking tray, pipe a thick circle of choux pastry 18 cm in diameter. Pipe a second, slightly smaller circle over it to form the complete ring. Glaze by brushing with the beaten egg. Scatter over flaked almonds. Bake for 1 hour.

Transfer to a rack and leave to cool. Leave the oven on. Make an 'inner tube' by piping a single circle of choux pastry the same size as the centre of the Paris-Brest. Glaze with the beaten egg and scatter over flaked almonds. Bake for 30 minutes. Leave to cool on a rack.

FOR THE FEUILLETINE PRALINE

Melt the milk chocolate, praline and butter over a bain-marie, stirring with a rubber palette knife. Add the pailleté feuilletine and mix until smooth. With a rolling pin, roll out the feuilletine praline between two sheets of baking parchment to a thickness of 4 mm. Chill in the freezer for 20 minutes. Use a knife to cut the cold feuilletine praline into 1-cm squares. Set aside in the freezer.

TIP

The 'inner tube' makes it possible to use less cream to make the Paris-Brest, making it much lighter.

FOR THE PARIS-BREST CREAM

In the mixer fitted with the whisk, beat the butter on speed 4 for 3 minutes until soft and creamy. Set aside. Whisk the very cold pastry cream in the mixer until smooth. Add the softened butter and praline. Whisk briskly to a very creamy consistency. Transfer to a piping bag fitted with a star nozzle.

ASSEMBLY AND FINISHING

Use a serrated knife to cut through the now well-dried choux ring at two-thirds of its height. Using a pastry ring or pastry cutter of the same diameter to trim the top part into a neat circle. Cut the 'inner tube' into two half circles to adjust it to the size of the crown. Trim the edges with a small paring knife.

Pipe a 1-cm-thick layer of Paris-Brest cream over the base of the ring. Arrange the 'inner tube' on top of the cream. Mask both inside and out by piping flame-like vertical lines of cream over it.

On the still-visible top part, arrange squares of feuilletine praline. Pipe a ring of cream over them, forming swirls. Arrange a few gold sugar almonds on the Paris-Brest cream to decorate. Put the cap in place, pressing lightly, and dust with icing sugar using a small sieve.

FRAMBOISIER ENTREMETS

FOR THE DIPLOMAT CREAM

Soften the gelatine leaves in a bowl of cold water. Combine the milk, scraped vanilla seeds and half the sugar in a saucepan over the heat. In a bowl, blanch the egg yolks by whisking them with the remaining sugar until thick and pale. Mix in the custard powder. When the milk comes to the boil, mix a small amount into the blanched egg yolks. Then return the mixture to the pan. Cook over a low heat, stirring constantly, for 4 minutes, until the cream thickens. Mix in the softened and drained gelatine. Transfer to a large dish and cover with cling film in direct contact. Set aside for about 1 hour in the refrigerator or 20 minutes in the freezer.

FOR THE ALMOND DACQUOISE

Preheat the oven to 160°C (Gas Mark 3). Sift the icing sugar, flour and ground almonds together through a fine sieve. In the mixer fitted with the whisk, start beating the egg whites, increasing the speed gradually until they form soft peaks. Then gradually add the caster sugar while beating to stiff peaks.
Fold the sifted powders into the beaten egg whites with a rubber palette knife. Transfer the dacquoise mixture to a piping bag fitted with a plain nozzle. Pipe the mixture in a spiral to make two discs of 16 cm in diameter. Scatter over the flaked almonds. Bake for 20 minutes.

ASSEMBLING AND FINISHING

Finish making the diplomat cream: whisk the whipping cream in the mixer fitted with the whisk on speed 8, then incorporate it into the pastry cream after whisking smooth. Use half the cream to fill a piping bag fitted with a plain nozzle.
Line the sides of an 18-cm-diameter entremets tart ring with a strip of acetate, then use a palette knife to apply a thin layer of diplomat cream over the acetate. Lightly trim the edges of the dacquoise discs to make neat and exactly 16 cm in diameter. Place the first dacquoise disc in the centre of the entremets ring. Pipe the diplomat cream in a spiral to cover the entire disc. Cover the cream completely with raspberries with their holes facing downwards.

FOR THE DIPLOMAT CREAM

3 gelatine leaves (6 g)

350 g milk

1 vanilla pod, split and scraped

50 g caster sugar

60 g (3) egg yolks

35 g custard powder

380 g whipping cream

FOR THE ALMOND DACQUOISE

150 g icing sugar

30 g plain flour

120 g ground almonds

150 g (5) egg whites

150 g caster sugar

50 g flaked almonds

FINISHING

250 g raspberries

30 g neutral glaze

40 g dessicated coconut

10 g icing sugar

30 g raspberry coulis

Mint leaves

VARIATIONS

You can vary by using other red berries, such as strawberries, wild strawberries, cherries, etc.

**Makes
1 entremets
(18 cm in
diameter)**

**Preparation
time:
1 hour
30 minutes**

**Cooking time:
20 minutes**

**Resting time:
3 hours–
3 hours
40 minutes**

Apply a thin layer of diplomat cream and smooth with a palette knife. Place the second dacquoise disc on top, pressing down lightly. Add a final thin layer of diplomatic cream, smoothing well with the palette knife so that it is at the same height as the top of the entremets ring.

Pipe mounds of diplomat cream in a circle around the edge of the entremets. Chill for 40 minutes in the freezer.

Remove the entremets ring. Brush a thin coating of neutral glaze around the sides of the entremets, then coat with the desiccated coconut. Fill the centre of the entremets with raspberries. Decorate with a few raspberries filled with raspberry coulis and others dipped in icing sugar. Add a few mint leaves. Dust the edge with icing sugar through a small sieve.

Chill in the refrigerator for 2 hours before serving.

RASPBERRY PROFITEROLES

FOR THE CHOUX PASTRY
Preheat the oven to 165°C (Gas Mark 3¼).
Make the choux pastry as described on p. 14 using the ingredients and quantities given here.
Transfer to a piping bag fitted with a plain nozzle. Pipe choux buns 4–5 cm in diameter on a baking tray, then score them with a fork. Bake for 35–40 minutes.

FOR THE MASCARPONE CHANTILLY CREAM
In the mixer fitted with the whisk, whisk the chilled cream with the mascarpone and scraped vanilla seeds on speed 8. When soft peaks form, add the icing sugar. Whisk again until the cream is fully whipped. Transfer to a piping bag fitted with a star nozzle.
Use a serrated knife to cut through the choux buns at two-thirds of their height. Using a 5-cm-diameter biscuit cutter to trim the caps into neat circles. Set aside.

FOR THE RASPBERRY COMPOTE
Combine the frozen raspberries and sugar in a saucepan. Mix with a rubber palette knife and bring to the boil. Cook over a high heat while stirring with a whisk. Check the temperature of the mixture with a cooking thermometer: the temperature should reach 104°C. Transfer to a dish and cover with cling film in direct contact. Refrigerate.
Once the compote is very cold, set aside 2 tablespoons for assembly and put the remaining compote in the mixer fitted with the pastry beater. Add the raspberries, lime juice and zest and mix on speed 2 for 2 minutes.

ASSEMBLY AND FINISHING
Fill the choux buns with raspberry compote. Pipe a good swirl of mascarpone Chantilly cream on top. Arrange raspberries in a circle around the cream. Grate the lime zest over the top. Place the caps on the profiteroles. Pipe a dot of compote on top of each one, then top with half a raspberry and dust the profiteroles with icing sugar using a small sieve.

FOR THE CHOUX PASTRY
75 g plain flour

125 g milk

50 g unsalted butter

5 g caster sugar

2 g salt

133 g (2 large or 3 small) eggs

1 beaten egg, for glazing

FOR THE MASCARPONE CHANTILLY CREAM
310 g whipping cream, chilled

180 g mascarpone cheese

2 vanilla pods, split and scraped

40 g icing sugar

FOR THE RASPBERRY COMPOTE
80 g frozen raspberries

80 g caster sugar

200 g raspberries

20 g lime juice

Zest of ½ lime

ASSEMBLY AND FINISHING
Icing sugar

200 g raspberries

Zest of 1 lime

TIP

If your kitchen is hot, don't hesitate to put the mixer bowl and whisk into the freezer for 30 minutes before whipping the Chantilly cream.

Makes
8 profiteroles

Preparation
time:
40 minutes

Cooking time:
50 minutes

CHOCOLATE RELIGIEUSE

FOR THE CHOUX PASTRY
75 g plain flour
125 g water
63 g unsalted butter
2 g caster sugar
2 g salt
150 g (3) eggs
1 beaten egg, for glazing

FOR THE PASTRY CREAM
500 g milk
1 vanilla pod, split and scraped
75 g caster sugar
100 g (5) egg yolks
45 g custard powder

FOR THE CHOCOLATE GANACHE
125 g whipping cream
95 g dark couverture chocolate (70%)

FOR THE CHOCOLATE BUTTERCREAM ICING
200 g caster sugar
240 g unsalted butter
50 g (1) egg
60 g (3) egg yolks
Cocoa paste (cacao liquor), depending on the desired colour

FINISHING
250 g sugar paste
Red food colouring
50 g cocoa paste
150 g chocolate buttercream icing (see above)
Edible gold leaf

Makes
8 religieuses

Preparation
time:
2 hours

Cooking time:
50–55
minutes

Resting time:
20 minutes–
1 hour

FOR THE CHOUX PASTRY

Preheat the oven to 150°C (Gas Mark 2). Make the choux pastry as described on p. 14 using the ingredients and quantities given here (see p. 188).
Transfer to a piping bag fitted with a plain nozzle. On a baking tray, pipe eight choux buns 5 cm in diameter and another eight 3 cm in diameter. Glaze the choux buns with beaten egg and score them with a fork.
Bake for 35–40 minutes.

FOR THE PASTRY CREAM

Combine the milk, scraped vanilla seeds and half the sugar in a saucepan over the heat. In a bowl, blanch the egg yolks by whisking them with the remaining sugar until thick and pale. Add the custard powder and mix again.
When the milk comes to the boil, mix a small amount into the blanched egg yolks. Then return the mixture to the pan. Cook over a low heat, stirring constantly, for 4 minutes, until the cream thickens. Transfer to a large dish and cover with cling film in direct contact. Set aside for about 1 hour in the refrigerator or 20 minutes in the freezer.

FOR THE CHOCOLATE GANACHE

In a saucepan, bring the cream to the boil. Pour the cream over the chocolate, either chopped or in drops (chips). Mix with a rubber palette knife.
Mix the ganache with the pastry cream, then transfer to a piping bag fitted with a nozzle. Refrigerate.

FOR THE CHOCOLATE BUTTERCREAM ICING

In a saucepan, combine 70 g of water with the sugar and place over the heat. Cut the butter into small pieces and leave it out of the refrigerator to soften.
In the mixer fitted with the whisk, whisk the egg and yolks on speed 4. When the temperature of the syrup reaches 121°C, reduce the mixer speed to 2 and pour the syrup over the eggs. Increase to speed 6 and continue to whisk until the mixture (pâte à bombe) starts to cool, then gradually reduce the speed to prevent the mixture collapsing. When the temperature reaches 29°C, gradually add the pieces of butter. Add the cocoa paste. Whisk the buttercream icing until smooth. Refrigerate. Transfer to a piping bag fitted with a 4-mm-diameter star nozzle.

INFO

You can find cocoa paste in specialist shops or on the internet.

FINISHING

Add a little hot water to the sugar paste to soften it, without stirring. Set aside while you fill the choux buns. Use a 4-mm-diameter star piping nozzle to pierce a hole, centred, in the bottom of each choux bun. Fill with chocolate pastry cream until it overflows. Use an angled palette knife to scrape off the excess.

Drain off the water from the sugar paste, then mix the paste with the food colouring and cocoa paste. It should be at a temperature of 37°C. Glaze each choux bun by dipping the top in the sugar paste. Remove the excess by wiping with your forefinger. Run your forefinger around the glaze to make it neat and stop it running down the sides.

Position the small choux buns on top of the large ones to form the religieuses. Place them on a rack. Pipe small flames of buttercream icing around each small choux bun. Finish decorating by piping a swirl of the icing on the top and applying gold leaf with a brush.

CARAMEL CHARLOTTE WITH PEARS

FOR THE CARAMEL BAVAROIS
Soften the gelatine leaves in a bowl of cold water. Heat the milk in a small saucepan. In another saucepan, make a dry caramel with 75 g of the sugar. Cook the sugar to a dark caramel. Deglaze the caramel by pouring in the hot milk.
In a large bowl, blanch the egg yolks by whisking them with the remaining sugar until thick and pale. Beat half the caramel milk, whisking constantly, into the blanched egg yolks. Pour the mixture back into the pan and put it back over the heat. Whisk briskly in a figure-of-eight motion. The resulting cream should be thick enough to coat a spoon.
Add the drained gelatine. Cool the mixture quickly by dipping the pan into a container filled with ice cubes. In the mixer fitted with the whisk, whip the cream to soft peaks on speed 8. When the mixture is at room temperature, fold in some of the whipped cream. When smooth, incorporate the remaining whipped cream.

FOR THE SPONGE
Preheat the oven to 190°C (Gas Mark 5). Sift the flour and whisk the egg yolks with the scraped vanilla seeds. In the mixer fitted with the whisk, beat the egg whites to soft peaks on speed 8, then gradually add the caster sugar while beating to stiff peaks. Use a rubber palette knife to mix the whisked egg yolks with the beaten egg whites. Gently fold in the sifted flour.
Transfer the mixture to a piping bag. On a baking tray lined with baking parchment, pipe a 5 x 22-cm strip of the mixture, one 20-cm-diameter disc and one 15-cm-diameter disc. Bake for 15–20 minutes.

FOR THE 30 BAUMÉ SYRUP
Put 100 g of water into a saucepan. Add the sugar and mix well to dissolve. Bring to the boil and cook until the sugar is fully dissolved.

FOR THE CARAMELISED PEARS
In a frying pan, make a dry caramel with the sugar. Cut the pears into cubes, add to the caramel and mix. Add the butter. The pears should be well coated. Transfer to a plate, cover and refrigerate.

FOR THE CARAMEL BAVAROIS
3 gelatine leaves (6 g)
200 g milk
165 g caster sugar
50 g (2 large) egg yolks
200 g whipping cream

FOR THE SPONGE
125 g plain flour
100 g (5) egg yolks
1 vanilla pod, split and scraped
150 g (5) egg whites
125 g caster sugar

FOR THE 30 BAUMÉ SYRUP
120 g caster sugar
20 g pear brandy

FOR THE CARAMELISED PEARS
100 g caster sugar
150 g pears in syrup
50 g unsalted butter

ASSEMBLY
300 g pears in syrup
Neutral glaze

Serves 8
(20 cm in
diameter)

Preparation
time:
1 hour
30 minutes

Cooking time:
30 minutes

Resting time:
1 hour

ASSEMBLY

Line the sides of an entremets ring with the sponge strip, trimming the ends if necessary so as not to overlap. Trim the large disc and position it inside the ring as a base. Brush the sponge with the Baumé syrup to soak.

Pipe a layer of caramel bavarois over the base. Cover with the pieces of very cold caramelised pear. Place the small sponge disc over them, pressing lightly. Brush with syrup to soak. Cover with caramel bavarois on top of the ring. Smooth with a palette knife and leave to set in the freezer for 1 hour. Slice the pears very thinly and arrange them in a rosette pattern covering the entire surface of the Charlotte. Cover the pears with a thin coating of somewhat runny glaze.

VANILLA AND CARAMEL MILLEFEUILLE

FOR THE PUFF PASTRY

Make the puff pastry as described on p. 17 using the quantities given here. Preheat the oven to 180°C (Gas Mark 4).

Roll out the pastry into a 70 x 25-cm rectangle with a thickness of 2 mm. Using a pastry ring and a knife, cut out three 20-cm diameter discs. Lay them on baking trays lined with baking parchment. Cover them with more baking parchment and a second baking tray. Put the trays into the oven to bake.

After 30 minutes, remove the top tray and baking parchment, then dust with icing sugar. Continue to bake for a further 10 minutes, until the pastry caramelises. Leave to cool on a rack. Use an 18-cm-diameter pastry ring to cut out discs with clean edges.

FOR THE MOUSSELINE CREAM

Combine the milk, scraped vanilla seeds and half the sugar in a saucepan over the heat. In a large bowl, blanch the eggs by whisking them with the remaining sugar until thick and pale. Add the custard powder and mix again.
When the milk comes to the boil, mix a small amount into the blanched eggs. Then return the mixture to the pan. Cook over a low heat, stirring constantly, for 4 minutes, until the cream thickens. Transfer to a large dish and cover with cling film in direct contact. Set aside for about 1 hour in the refrigerator or 20 minutes in the freezer.
In the mixer fitted with the whisk, beat the butter on speed 4 for 3 minutes, until soft and creamy. Set aside. Whisk the very cold pastry cream in the mixer until smooth. Add the softened butter. Whisk briskly to a very creamy consistency. Fill a piping bag fitted with a plain nozzle and refrigerate.

FOR THE CARAMEL CREAM

Soften the gelatine leaf in a bowl of cold water. In a saucepan, cook the sugar to a dry caramel. In another saucepan, combine the cream, glucose and scraped vanilla seeds and bring to the boil. Deglaze the caramel with the hot cream. Add the egg yolk and cook until the cream is thick enough to coat a spoon. Mix in the drained gelatine, transfer to a piping bag and leave to cool.

FOR THE PUFF PASTRY
375 g dry butter
250 g water
500 g plain flour
10 g salt

FOR THE MOUSSELINE CREAM
500 g milk
1 vanilla pod, split and scraped
60 g caster sugar
2 eggs
60 g custard powder
150 g unsalted butter, softened

FOR THE CARAMEL CREAM
1 gelatine leaf (2 g)
65 g caster sugar
110 g whipping cream
9 g glucose powder
1 vanilla pod
24 g (1 large) egg yolk

ASSEMBLY AND FINISHING
Icing sugar
1 almond

TIP

Assemble the millefeuille at the last minute so that the puff pastry remains crisp.

Serves 6
(18 cm in
diameter)

Preparation
time:
2 hours

Cooking time:
40 minutes

Resting time:
1 hour
45 minutes

ASSEMBLY AND FINISHING

Pipe mounds of mousseline cream all around the edge of first pastry disc, then pipe the cream in a spiral inside. Add a little caramel cream to the centre of the disc. Cover with a second pastry disc, pressing lightly. Repeat the piping process and finish with the final pastry disc

Using a round piece of card as a template, dust the top with icing sugar through a small sieve to create a crescent moon pattern. Decorate the top further with a dot of mousseline cream topped with an almond.

CITRUS BRIOCHE POLONAISE

FOR THE BRIOCHE DOUGH
200 g (4) eggs
15 g fresh yeast
330 g Italian '00' flour or plain flour
60 g caster sugar
7 g fine salt
170 g unsalted butter
Zest of 2 oranges
1 beaten egg, for glazing

FOR THE GRAND MARNIER® PASTRY CREAM
250 g full-fat milk
50 g unsalted butter
1 vanilla pod
25 g caster sugar
50 g (2 large) egg yolks
23 g cornflour
30 g Grand Marnier®

FOR THE SOAKING SYRUP
270 g caster sugar
Zest of 1 orange
50 g Grand Marnier®

FOR THE FILLING
50 g candied lemon peel cubes
50 g candied orange peel cubes
50 g candied citron peel cubes

FOR THE FRENCH MERINGUE
200 g icing sugar
250 g (8–9) egg whites
200 g caster sugar

FINISHING
Icing sugar
Orange slices
Candied orange peels
Verbena leafs

Makes
2 medium
brioches

Preparation
time:
1 hour
20 minutes

Cooking time:
35 minutes

Resting time:
5 hours
10 minutes

FOR THE DOUGH

Make the brioche dough as described on p. 14 using the ingredients and quantities given here (see p. 196).

RISING

Take the dough out of the mixer and shape it into a ball. Place it in a large bowl and cover with cling film in direct contact. Leave to rise at room temperature for 1 hour.

Deflate the dough, then shape it into a ball and wrap in cling film. Refrigerate for 2 hours.

FOR THE GRAND MARNIER® PASTRY CREAM

Put the milk, melted butter, scraped vanilla seeds and half the sugar into a saucepan and place over the heat. In a large bowl, blanch the egg yolks by whisking them with the remaining sugar until thick and pale. Mix in the cornflour. When the milk comes to the boil, mix a small amount into the blanched egg yolks. Return the mixture to the pan and cook, constantly stirring, over a low heat for 4 minutes.

Transfer the pastry cream to a dish, cover with cling film in direct contact and chill in the freezer for 15–20 minutes.

When cold, add the Grand Marnier® and refrigerate.

SHAPING

Deflate the dough, then divide and weigh it out into two portions of 350 g each. Shape the individual pieces into balls by rolling them with the palm of your hand on the work surface. Rest at room temperature for 5 minutes. Grease cake rings with butter and line with a strip of baking parchment. Place the rings on baking parchment. Put the dough balls into the centre of the cake rings and flatten with the back of your hand. Brush the top of the brioche with the beaten egg, taking care not to let any drip down the sides.

PROVING

Prove the brioches in an improvised proving oven at 24°C for 2 hours (see p. 24).

TIPS

You can also use stale brioches for this recipe. For greater precision when piping the pastry cream and meringue, if you have one, use a size 10 plain nozzle.

BAKING

Take the brioches out of the oven and rest at room temperature for 10 minutes. Preheat the oven to 190°C (Gas Mark 5) with the oven baking tray inside. Glaze the brioches again.
Place on the hot baking tray and bake at 170°C (Gas Mark 3½) for 20–25 minutes. Transfer to a rack and leave to cool.

FOR THE SOAKING SYRUP

In a saucepan, combine 300 g of water with the sugar and grated orange zest, and bring to the boil. Leave the syrup to cool completely, then add the Grand Marnier®. Set aside at room temperature.

FILLING

Use a serrated knife to cut horizontally through the brioche to make three discs. Brush each of the discs with the syrup to soak.
Smooth the pastry cream in a large bowl. Transfer to a piping bag and fill the brioche. Start by covering the bottom disc with pastry cream. Sprinkle with cubes of candied lemon, candied orange and candied citron. Cover with the second brioche disc and fill again with pastry cream and candied citrus cubes. Cover with the top disc. Clean the sides of the brioche, leaving smooth. Refrigerate.

FOR THE FRENCH MERINGUE

Sift the icing sugar through a fine sieve over baking parchment. In the mixer fitted with the whisk, whisk the egg whites on speed 8. When soft peaks form, gradually add the caster sugar while beating to stiff peaks. Fold in the icing sugar with a rubber palette knife.

FINISHING

Transfer the meringue to a piping bag. Pipe meringue over the pastry cream-filled brioche. Dust with icing sugar. Transfer the brioche to the oven baking tray. Toast the meringue in the hot oven at 200°C (Gas Mark 6) for 5–10 minutes. Transfer to a rack and leave to cool. Decorate with an orange slice, a slice of candied orange peel and a verbena leaf.

YUZU TARTLETS

FOR THE YUZU CREAM
The previous day – or a few hours in advance – bring water to a simmer in a large saucepan. Beat the eggs with the sugar in a smaller saucepan, then add the crème fraîche and the yuzu juice. Place the smaller saucepan inside the larger one and whisk the mixture continuously for 15 minutes, until the cream thickens. When the cream is cooked, transfer to a glass jar and leave to cool. Refrigerate for 12 hours.

FOR THE SWEET SHORTCRUST PASTRY
On the actual day, make the pastry as described on p. 15 using the ingredients and quantities given here.

SHAPING AND BAKING
Preheat the oven to 180°C (Gas Mark 4). On a floured work surface, roll out the dough to a thickness of 4 mm with a rolling pin. Using an upside-down tartlet tin as a template and leaving a 2–3-cm margin, cut out 10 discs from the pastry. Grease the tartlet tins with butter and line with the pastry discs. Prick the tartlet cases with a fork and bake 12–15 minutes. Leave to cool on a rack and then fill with the yuzu cream. Refrigerate until it is time to serve.

FOR THE YUZU CREAM
3 eggs
100 g caster sugar
100 g crème fraîche
100 ml yuzu juice

FOR THE SWEET SHORTCRUST PASTRY
150 g unsalted butter, softened
100 g icing sugar
50 g ground almonds
1 small egg, beaten
300 g plain flour

TIPS

Decorate with grated lime zest. You can find yuzu juice in Japanese and Asian food shops.

Makes

10 tartlets

Preparation time:
30 minutes

Cooking time:
30 minutes

Resting time:
13 hours

SCHUSS CHEESECAKE

FOR THE BRETON SHORTBREAD PASTRY
25 g (1 large) egg yolk
50 g brown sugar
65 g semi-salted butter
65 g organic plain flour
3 g baking powder
1 pinch fleur de sel

FOR THE BISCUIT VIENNOIS
12 g (½) egg yolk
30 g caster sugar
90 g ground almonds
35 g (1 small) egg
85 g (3 small) egg whites
35 g plain flour

FOR THE STRAWBERRY JELLY
5 g gelatine
250 g strawberry purée

FOR THE 30 BAUMÉ STRAWBERRY SYRUP
340 g caster sugar
Strawberry purée, to taste

FOR THE FROMAGE BLANC MOUSSE
3½ gelatine leaves (7 g)
40 g (2) egg yolks
55 g caster sugar
1 vanilla pod
170 g fromage blanc (40% fat)
210 g soft-whipped cream

FOR THE MASCARPONE CHANTILLY CREAM
125 g whipping cream
15 g icing sugar
70 g mascarpone cheese

DECORATION
250 g strawberries
60 g blackberries
125 g raspberries
60 g blueberries
Red cocoa powder (optional)

or

Makes
1 entremets
(16 cm in
diameter)

Preparation
time:
1 hour
30 minutes

Cooking time:
30 minutes

Resting time:
2 hours

SCHUSS
CHEESECAKE

FOR THE BRETON SHORTBREAD PASTRY

Make the Breton shortbread pastry by following the instructions described on p. 15 using the ingredients and quantities given here (see p. 202).

Wrap in cling film and refrigerate for at least 1 hour.

Preheat the oven to 180°C (Gas Mark 4). Use a 16-cm-diameter pastry ring to make a shortbread disc of the same size. Bake at 170°C (Gas Mark 3½) for 12–15 minutes, until golden.

Wait 5 minutes before lifting off the ring, then leave to cool on a rack.

FOR THE BISCUIT VIENNOIS

Preheat the oven to 200°C (Gas Mark 6).

In the mixer fitted with the whisk, add the egg yolk with half the sugar and the ground almonds. Mix on speed 4, gradually adding the whole egg and beat for about 10 minutes to a ribbon consistency. Transfer to a large bowl and wash the mixer bowl.

In the mixer fitted with the whisk, add the egg whites and the remaining sugar and whisk on speed 8 to stiff peaks. Gently fold into the previous mixture. Incorporate the sifted flour.

Line a 52 x 32-cm baking tray with baking parchment. Spread the batter over the baking tray with an angled palette knife. Bake for 10 minutes. Then transfer immediately to a rack to cool quickly without drying out. Leave to cool to room temperature, then cut out two 16-cm-diameter sponge discs. Refrigerate.

FOR THE STRAWBERRY JELLY

Soften the gelatine in a large bowl filled with cold water. In a saucepan, heat the strawberry purée to a maximum temperature of 55–60°C. Drain the gelatine and add it to the purée. Mix with a whisk to dissolve the gelatine. Pour into a 16-cm-diameter round mould. Freeze for about 1 hour.

FOR THE 30 BAUMÉ STRAWBERRY SYRUP

Put 250 g of water into a saucepan. Add the sugar and mix well. Bring to the boil until the sugar is fully dissolved. Mix in the strawberry purée. Set aside.

Special
occasions

INFO

You can find coloured cocoa in specialist shops or on the Internet.

FOR THE FROMAGE BLANC MOUSSE

Soften the gelatine in a bowl of cold water. In the mixer fitted with a whisk, combine the egg yolks with half of the sugar and beat on speed 8.

In a saucepan, heat the remaining sugar and 20 g water to 120°C. Pour the syrup over the egg yolks and whisk until the mixture (pâte à bombe) cools to room temperature.

Scrape the vanilla pod and add the seeds to the fromage blanc. Drain and melt the gelatine in a saucepan over a low heat. Mix a quarter of the fromage blanc with the melted gelatine. Transfer to a large bowl and add the remaining fromage blanc. With a rubber palette knife, gently fold in the pâte à bombe, followed by the soft-whipped cream.

ASSEMBLY

Line an entremets ring with an acetate strip and cover with a thin layer of the fromage blanc mousse. Position the Breton shortbread disc at the bottom of the ring. Use a palette knife to cover the shortbread entirely with fromage blanc mousse.

Place the first biscuit viennois sponge disc in the ring. Soak the sponge with the strawberry syrup. Use a piping bag to apply a spiral of fromage blanc mousse over the soaked sponge, covering it completely. Position the still-frozen jelly disc on top. Pipe more fromage blanc mousse over the jelly to cover it completely. Place the second sponge disc on top, pressing lightly, then soak with the strawberry syrup.

Add another layer of fromage blanc mousse, smoothing with a palette knife to make the same height as the entremets ring. Freeze for 40 minutes.

FOR THE MASCARPONE CHANTILLY CREAM

Make the cream as described on p. 186.

Remove the ring from the entremets and pipe Chantilly cream over the top. Place in the freezer for 15 minutes, then spray the still-frozen entremets with red cocoa powder. Decorate the dessert with the mixed berries.

CHOCOLATE AND PRALINE
YULE LOG

FOR THE CHOCOLATE AND PRALINE GANACHE

Melt the chocolate. In a saucepan, heat the cream with the praline. Pour the mixture over the chocolate, a third at a time, mixing well with a rubber palette knife each time. Mix in the crushed caramelised nuts. Cover with cling film in direct contact and set aside at room temperature.

FOR THE SPONGE CAKE

Preheat the oven to 180°C (Gas Mark 4). In the mixer fitted with the whisk, add the sugar, eggs and vanilla extract. Whisk on speed 8 for 5 minutes, until the mixture doubles in volume. Sprinkle the flour and baking powder over the mixture and gently fold in with a rubber palette knife. Spread the mixture into a rectangle of about 25 x 30 cm on a baking tray lined with baking parchment, then smooth with a palette knife for a uniform thickness. Bake for 10–12 minutes, then leave to cool. Moisten a clean cloth with water, cover the sponge and then turn it over. Peel off the baking parchment and then roll up the sponge sheet in the cloth. Leave to cool.

ASSEMBLY

When the sponge is cold, unroll it and cover the entire surface with ganache. Roll it up again tightly, then wrap in cling film. Refrigerate for 2 hours.

FOR THE ROCHER GLAZE

Melt the chocolate, add the oil and mix well. Mix in the chopped almonds. Unwrap the log and trim off the ends cleanly. Place the log on a rack set over a plate, then pour over the glaze, covering the cake completely. Carefully transfer to a dish and refrigerate until ready to serve.

FOR THE CHOCOLATE AND PRALINE GANACHE

200 g dark chocolate

90 g whipping cream

3 tbsp praline

2 tbsp crushed caramelised almonds or hazelnuts

FOR THE SPONGE CAKE

90 g caster sugar

4 eggs

1 tsp vanilla extract

100 g plain flour

½ tsp baking powder

FOR THE ROCHER GLAZE

200 g milk chocolate

35 g grapeseed oil

50 g chopped almonds

ALMOND AND RASPBERRY
GALETTE
DES ROIS

FOR THE PUFF PASTRY
Make the puff pastry as described on p. 17 using the quantities given here.
Cut out two discs 28 cm in diameter. Leave them in the refrigerator while you make the filling.

FOR THE ALMOND CREAM
In the mixer fitted with the pastry beater, combine the ground almonds, sugar, apple sauce, eggs and bitter almond essence on speed 1 for 3 minutes.

ASSEMBLY
Spread the almond cream over a puff pastry disc, leaving a 2-cm border around the edges. Scatter the frozen raspberries over the cream. Press the bean deep into the almond cream. Moisten the uncovered edge of the pastry with a little water, then cover with the second disc. Use your hands to seal the two discs together, pressing to where the filling ends. Crimp the edges by lightly pressing around the pastry with the back of a knife to ensure that the two discs will remain attached when baked. Make a small hole in the centre of the pie to allow steam to escape. You can use a knife tip to decorate the surface of the pie. Use a fork to beat the remaining egg with a teaspoon of water. Brush the pastry with the egg wash, leaving the sides free. Refrigerate for at least 2 hours.

BAKING
Preheat the oven to 200°C (Gas Mark 6). Glaze the pie again with beaten egg. Bake for about 25 minutes. Leave to cool before serving.

FOR THE PUFF PASTRY
500 g plain flour
½ tsp salt
120 g water
180 g unsalted butter

FOR THE ALMOND CREAM
160 g ground almonds
100 g caster sugar
100 g apple sauce
2 eggs + 1 egg, for glazing
1 tsp bitter almond essence

ASSEMBLY
70 g frozen raspberries
1 bean

VARIATIONS

To make a classic frangipane cream, first make a pastry cream (see p. 19), doubling the quantities of the basic recipe. Leave to cool. Then make an almond cream by mixing 100 g of softened butter, 100 g of sugar, 100 g of ground almonds and 1 egg in the mixer fitted with the pastry beater on speed 1 for 2 minutes. Incorporate the cooled pastry cream, then fill the puff pastry discs with the cream.

Serves 8–10

Preparation
time:
55 minutes

Cooking time:
25 minutes

Resting time:
4 hours

APPENDICES

TABLE OF CONTENTS

INDEX BY RECIPE TYPE

INDEX BY INGREDIENT

Appendices

OTHER ACCESSORIES FOR THE ARTISAN MIXER

You can find all the accessories for the KitchenAid Artisan mixer in the book *KitchenAid, for Everything You Want to Make*, released in 2018:

FOR CULINARY PREPARATIONS

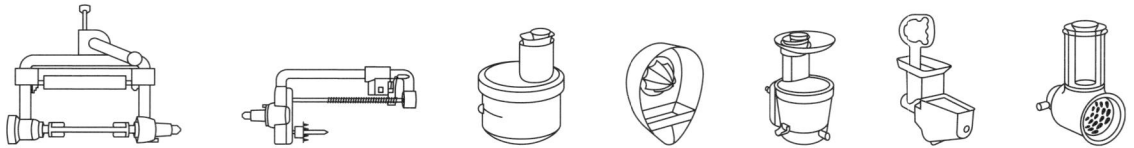

- Vegetable Sheet Cutter
- Spiralizer with Peel, Core and Slice
- Food Processor Attachment
- Citrus Juicer
- Slow Juicer and Sauce Attachment
- Food Strainer
- Vegetable Slicer and Shaver

FOR PASTA AND GRAINS

- Pasta Sheet Roller and Cutter Set
- Ravioli Maker
- Pasta Dryer
- Grain Mill

FOR MEAT-BASED SAVOURY DISHES

- Metal Food Grinder
- Food Grinder
- Sausage Stuffer

FOR SWEET TREATS

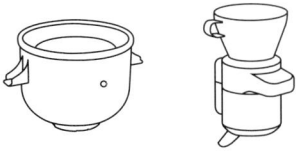

- Ice Cream Maker
- Sifter and Scale Attachment

ACKNOWLEDGEMENTS
To all the Passionate Makers who have inspired us since 1919.
KitchenAid Europa, Inc. Nijverheidslaan 3, box 5, 1853 Strombeek-Bever, Belgium
https://www.kitchenaid.eu/

MANAGING DIRECTOR
Aurore Charoy

EDITORS
Élise Labry, Fanny Morgensztern and Jessica Rostain, assisted by Aude Letorey

LAYOUT AND PHOTOENGRAVING
Nord Compo

PHOTOGRAPHY
Rina Nurra, Françoise Nicol, Thomas Dhellemmes, Valéry Guedes, Laurent Dequick, Amélie Roche and Édouard Sicot

ENGLISH TRANSLATION
Cillero & de Motta

Printed in Spain by Ingoprint.

ISBN: 978-2-38184-028-4
Legal deposit: 3rd quarter 2021

© Webedia Books 2021
Webedia Books
2, rue Paul-Vaillant-Couturier
92300 Levallois-Perret